SPECTRUM

Test Prep

Grade 4

Published by Spectrum
an imprint of Carson-Dellosa Publishing LLC
Greensboro, NC

Spectrum
An imprint of Carson-Dellosa Publishing LLC
P.O. Box 35665
Greensboro, NC 27425 USA

Printed in Mayfield, PA USA • All rights reserved.   ISBN 0-7696-8624-9

7 8 9 10 11 12 PAH 14 13 12 11 10   181108091

Table of Contents

What's Inside? 5

English Language Arts

Standards and What They Mean 7

Reading and Comprehension
Comparing Story Elements 9
Read and Respond to Fiction 10
Read and Respond to Nonfiction 11
Identifying Literature Genres 12
Responding to Literature 14
Identifying Textual Features 15
Evaluating Information 16
Determining Meaning Using Context 17
Mini-Test 1 . . . . **18**

Writing
Using Words Correctly 19
Varying Sentence Structure 20
Identifying Types of Sentences 21
Using an Organizational Structure 22
Writing With Details 23
Writing a Persuasive Essay 24
Writing a Narrative Procedure 25
Spelling 26
Capitalization and Punctuation 27
Using Figurative Language 28
Mini-Test 2 . . . . **29**

Research
Analyzing Informational Reports 30
Using a Dictionary 31
Using Resources 32
Mini-Test 3 . . . . **33**

Cultural and Social Language Use
Identifying Cultural Language Use 34
Sharing a Book Review 35
Writing a Personal Narrative 36
Mini-Test 4 . . . . **37**

How Am I Doing? **38**

Final English Language Arts Test **40**
Answer Sheet 43

Mathematics

Standards and What They Mean **44**

Number and Operations
Using Whole Numbers and
Expanded Notation 45
Using Fractions and Number Lines 46
Factors and Multiples 47
Multiplication and Division 48
Addition and Subtraction 49

Algebra
Identifying and Extending Patterns 50
Working With Variables 51
Commutative and Associative Properties . . . 52
Using Data to Draw Conclusions 53
Quantity and Change 54
Mini-Test 1 . . . . **55**

Geometry
Identifying Quadrilaterals 56
Identifying Triangles 57
Using Coordinates 58
Lines of Symmetry and Rotational
Symmetry 59
Using Geometric Shapes 60

Measurement
Selecting Units of Measure 61
Converting U.S. Customary Measurements . 62
Finding the Perimeter 63
Finding the Volume 64
Mini-Test 2 . . . . **65**

Data Analysis and Probability
Representing Data 66
Describing and Comparing Data 67
Developing and Testing Predictions 68
Determining Likelihood of Outcomes 69

Process
Solving Problems 70
Evaluating Mathematical Arguments 71
Using Mathematical Language 72
Connecting and Representing
Mathematical Ideas 73
Mini-Test 3 . . . . **74**

How Am I Doing? **75**

Final Mathematics Test **76**
Answer Sheet 79

Social Studies

Standards and What They Mean **80**

Culture
  Expressions of Culture 81
  Men, Women, and Children in Societies . . . 82
Time, Continuity, and Change
  Using Time Lines 83
  Different Perspectives on Historical Events . 84
People, Places, and Environment
  Geographic Regions of Earth 85
  Effect of Physical Processes on the Earth . . 86
  Environmental Patterns 87
  Mini-Test 1 . . . . **88**
Individual Development and Identity
  Making Connections to Places 89
  Identifying the Impact of Groups 90
Individuals, Groups, and Institutions
  Individuals, Groups, and Institutions
    in Society 91
  Mini-Test 2 . . . . **93**
Powers, Authority, and Governance
  Levels and Branches of Government 94
  Identifying Powers of the National
    Government 95
Production, Distribution, and Consumption
  Factors Affecting Consumer Choice 96
  Supply, Demand, and Price 97
Science, Technology, and Society
  American Inventors 98
  Protecting the Environment 99
  Mini-Test 3 . . . . **100**
Global Connections
  Global Warming 101
Civic Ideals and Practices
  Rights and Responsibilities of Citizens . . . 103
  Natural Rights 104
  Mini-Test 4 . . . . **105**
How Am I Doing? **106**
Final Social Studies Test **108**
  Answer Sheet 111

Science

Standards and What They Mean **112**

Unifying Concepts and Processes
  Confirming Hypotheses 114
Science as Inquiry
  Scientific Inquiry 115
  Scientific Results and Knowledge 116
  Mini-Test 1 . . . . **117**
Physical Science
  Properties of Matter 118
  Types of Motion 119
  Forms of Energy 120
Life Science
  Organisms in Ecosystems 121
  Factors Affecting Life Spans/Life Cycles . . 122
Earth and Space Science
  Patterns in the Solar System 123
  Properties of Water 124
  Weather 125
  Earth's Processes 126
  Mini-Test 2 . . . . **127**
Science and Technology
  Use of Technology in Science 128
Science in Personal and Social Perspectives
  Nutrition and Exercise 129
History and Nature of Science
  Famous Scientists 130
  Mini-Test 3 . . . . **131**
How Am I Doing? **132**
Final Science Test **133**
  Answer Sheet 136

Answer Key **137**

What's Inside?

This workbook is designed to help you and your fourth grader understand what he or she will be expected to know on standardized tests.

Practice Pages

The workbook is divided into four sections: English Language Arts, Mathematics, Social Studies, and Science. The practice activities in this workbook provide students with practice in each of these areas. Each section has practice activities that have questions similar to those that will appear on the standardized tests. Students should use a pencil to fill in the correct answers and to complete any writing on these activities.

National Standards

Before each practice section is a list of the national standards covered by that section. These standards list the knowledge and skills that students are expected to master at each grade level. The shaded *What it means* sections will help to explain any information in the standards that might be unfamiliar.

Mini-Tests and Final Tests

When your student finishes the practice pages for specific standards, your student can move on to a mini-test that covers the material presented on those practice activities. After an entire set of standards and accompanying practice pages are completed, your student should take the final tests, which incorporate materials from all the practice pages in that section.

Final Test Answer Sheet

The final tests have separate answer sheets that mimic the style of the answer sheets the students will use on the standardized tests. The answer sheets appear at the end of each final test.

How Am I Doing?

The *How Am I Doing?* pages are designed to help students identify areas where they are proficient and areas where they still need more practice. They will pinpoint areas where more work is needed as well as areas where your student excels. Students can keep track of each of their mini-test scores on these pages.

Answer Key

Answers to all the practice pages, mini-tests, and final tests are listed by page number and appear at the end of the book.

To find a complete listing of the national standards in each subject area, you can access the following Web sites:

The National Council of Teachers of English: www.ncte.org
National Council of Teachers of Mathematics: www.nctm.org/standards
National Council for the Social Studies: www.ncss.org/standards
National Science Teachers Association: www.nsta.org/standards

English Language Arts Standards

Standard 1 *(See pages 9–11.)*
Students read a wide range of print and nonprint texts to build an understanding of texts, of themselves, and of the cultures of the United States and the world; to acquire new information; to respond to the needs and demands of society and the workplace; and for personal fulfillment. Among these texts are fiction and nonfiction, classic and contemporary works.

Standard 2 *(See pages 12–14.)*
Students read a wide range of literature from many periods in many genres to build an understanding of the many dimensions (e.g., philosophical, ethical, aesthetic) of human experience.

What it means:
- Genre is the type or category of literature. Some examples of genres include fiction, nonfiction, biographies, poetry, and fables. Each genre is categorized by various differences in form. For example, nonfiction differs from fiction in that it presents facts or tells a true story. The fable differs from the broader category of fiction because it has a moral or character lesson.

Standard 3 *(See pages 15–17.)*
Students apply a wide range of strategies to comprehend, interpret, evaluate, and appreciate texts. They draw on their prior experience, their interactions with other readers and writers, their knowledge of word meaning and of other texts, their word identification strategies, and their understanding of textual features (e.g., sound-letter correspondence, sentence structure, context, graphics).

What it means:
- Students should be able to use several different strategies to help them determine the meaning of unfamiliar words.

Standard 4 *(See pages 19–21.)*
Students adjust their use of spoken, written, and visual language (e.g., conventions, style, vocabulary) to communicate effectively with a variety of audiences and for different purposes.

Standard 5 *(See pages 21–25.)*
Students employ a wide range of strategies as they write and use different writing process elements appropriately to communicate with different audiences for a variety of purposes.

Standard 6 *(See pages 26–28.)*
Students apply knowledge of language structure, language conventions (e.g., spelling and punctuation), media techniques, figurative language, and genre to create, critique, and discuss print and nonprint texts.

What it means:
- Figurative language is language used for descriptive effect. It describes or implies meaning, rather than stating it directly. Similes, metaphors, hyperboles, and personification are types of figurative language.

English Language Arts Standards

Standard 7 *(See page 30.)*
Students conduct research on issues and interests by generating ideas and questions, and by posing problems. They gather, evaluate, and synthesize data from a variety of sources (e.g., print and nonprint texts, artifacts, people) to communicate their discoveries in ways that suit their purpose and audience.

Standard 8 *(See pages 31–32.)*
Students use a variety of technological and informational resources (e.g., libraries, databases, computer networks, video) to gather and synthesize information and to create and communicate knowledge.

Standard 9 *(See page 34.)*
Students develop an understanding of and respect for diversity in language use, patterns, and dialects across cultures, ethnic groups, geographic regions, and social roles.

Standard 10
Students whose first language is not English make use of their first language to develop competency in the English language arts and to develop understanding of content across the curriculum.

Standard 11 *(See page 35.)*
Students participate as knowledgeable, reflective, creative, and critical members of a variety of literacy communities.

Standard 12 *(See page 36.)*
Students use spoken, written, and visual language to accomplish their own purposes (e.g., for learning, enjoyment, persuasion, and the exchange of information).

English Language Arts

1.0

Comparing Story Elements
Reading and Comprehension

DIRECTIONS: The following stories were written by the same person. Read both stories, then fill in the blank with the correct answer from the parentheses.

> Maggie and Isabel went to the park on Saturday. They both headed for the slides. But they couldn't decide who should go first. Isabel said she should because she was older. Maggie said she should go first because Isabel always got to. Just then, their mother came over and said, "Why don't you each get on one slide and start down at the same time?"
>
> That's just what they did.

> Joel's hockey team had been playing well all season, and this was their chance to win the tournament. He was their best player.
>
> He glanced around at his teammates. "Guys," he said. "Let's skate really hard and show them how great we are!"
>
> The team cheered and started to walk out to the ice. Joel turned around to grab his helmet, but it wasn't there. He looked under the benches and in the lockers, but his helmet wasn't anywhere. He sat down and felt his throat get tight. If he didn't have a helmet, he couldn't play.
>
> Just then, there was a knock on the door. Joel's mom peeked her head around the locker room door. "Thank goodness," she said. "I got here just in time with your helmet."

1. **Both of the stories are** _____ .

   (fiction / nonfiction)

2. **Both stories are about** _____
   that gets solved.

   (an argument / a problem)

3. **The person who solves the problem in both**
   stories is _____ .

   (the coach / the mother)

4. **If both of these stories appeared together in a**
   book of similar stories, a good title for the
   book would be _____ .

   (Sports Bloopers / Mom to the Rescue)

5. **The author's purpose for writing both stories**
   is to _____ .

   (A) entertain the reader

   (B) alarm the reader

   (C) inform the reader

   (D) challenge the reader

English Language Arts

Read and Respond to Fiction
Reading and Comprehension

DIRECTIONS: Read the passage and answer the questions that follow.

A Bumpy Ride

When we first climbed into the car and strapped on our safety belts, I wasn't very nervous. I was sitting right next to my big brother and he had done this many times before. As we started to climb the hill, however, I could feel my heart jump into my throat. "Brian?" I asked nervously. "Is this supposed to be so noisy?" "Sure, Matthew," Brian answered. "It always does that." A minute later, we were going so fast down the hill I didn't have time to think. With a twist, a loop, and a bunch of fast turns, everyone on board screamed in delight. No wonder this was one of the most popular rides in the park. By the time the car pulled into the station and we got off the ride, I was ready to do it again!

1. Which of the following is a characteristic of fiction?

- (A) It provides facts.
- (B) It tells a story.
- (C) It is real and true.
- (D) It informs the reader.

2. Which of the following best describes the setting of this story?

- (F) a car ride to school
- (G) a train ride
- (H) a ride on a roller coaster
- (J) a trip to the grocery store

3. What might have happened if this story had taken place in a regular car?

- (A) Brian might have lost his license for careless driving.
- (B) Brian might have started a taxi business.
- (C) Matthew might have wanted to drive with Brian again.
- (D) Matthew might not have been nervous.

4. At what point in the story did you realize where it was taking place? What words or phrases helped you figure out the setting?

_____

_____

_____

_____

_____

_____

_____

_____

_____

_____

_____

_____

_____

Name _____ Date _____

Read and Respond to Nonfiction
Reading and Comprehension

DIRECTIONS: Read the passage and answer the questions that follow.

Have you ever seen someone send a code for SOS? Maybe you've seen an old movie showing a ship about to sink. Perhaps someone on the ship was tapping wildly on a device. That person was using the telegraph to send for help.

Samuel Morse invented the telegraph. He also invented the electronic alphabet called *Morse code.* The code was a set of dots and dashes that stood for each number and letter of the alphabet.

In 1832, Morse was sailing back to the United States from Europe. During the trip, he came up with the idea of an electronic telegraph. It would help people communicate across great distances. They would be able to be in contact with each other from ship to shore. He was eager to make his invention as quickly as possible.

By 1835, he had made his first telegraph. However, it was only a trial version. In 1844, he built a telegraph line. It went from Baltimore to Washington, D.C. The telegraph line was like a telephone line today. It carried Morse code messages from one person to another.

Morse kept working to make his telegraph better. In 1849, the government gave him a patent. This gave him the right to make his invention. Within a few years, there were 23,000 miles of telegraph wire. People could now communicate across great distances.

As a result of his invention, trains ran more safely. Conductors could warn about dangers or problems and ask for help. People in businesses could communicate more easily. This made it easier to sell their goods and services. Morse had changed communication forever.

1. What is the main idea of this passage?

_____

_____

_____

2. Give three details from the passage that helped you answer Question 1.

_____

_____

_____

3. What type of writing is this passage?

(A) fiction

(B) poetry

(C) nonfiction

(D) fable

4. What was the author's purpose for writing this passage?

(F) to entertain the reader

(G) to alarm the reader

(H) to inform the reader

(J) to challenge the reader

English Language Arts

Identifying Literature Genres
Reading and Comprehension

DIRECTIONS: Read the passage and answer the questions that follow.

A **genre** is a type of literature. There are several different kinds of literature. Some examples of literature include:
- A **biography,** which is a story that gives details about a real person's life.
- A **fable,** which is a story that teaches a moral, or lesson. It often has animal characters.
- A **poem,** which is a short piece of writing set up in lines. It often has a rhythm and words that rhyme.

In 1908, Jacqueline Cochran was born to a poor family in Florida. Like many girls at the time, she went to work at an early age. When she was just eight years old, she started work in a cotton mill. As she made cloth, she dreamed about becoming a pilot. She wanted to fly one of the planes that had been recently invented.

Jacqueline got her wish in the 1930s. At this time, only a few daring young men flew these new planes. There were very few women pilots. That did not stop Jacqueline. She took flying lessons and became a pilot. She began to enter famous races. In 1938, she won first prize in a contest to fly across the United States.

At the beginning of World War II, Jacqueline trained women in England as pilots. She later came back to the United States and trained American women, too. In 1945, she was given the Distinguished Service Medal. It is one of America's highest honors.

When jet planes were invented, Jacqueline learned to fly them, too. She was the first woman to fly faster than the speed of sound. She also set many other records, including flying higher than anyone had before her.

In many ways, Jacqueline is forgotten today. But she was a pioneer in a new technology. She helped to make air travel one of our most important means of transportation.

1. **This passage is which genre, or type of literature?**
   - (A) fiction
   - (B) poetry
   - (C) biography
   - (D) fable

2. **What clues in the passage helped you decide what genre it is?**

   _____

   _____

   _____

   _____

   _____

   _____

   _____

GO

DIRECTIONS: Read the passage and answer the questions that follow.

Fox and the Grapes

One warm summer day, a fox was walking along when he noticed a bunch of grapes on a vine above him. Cool, juicy grapes would taste so good. The more he thought about it, the more the fox wanted those grapes. He tried standing on his tiptoes. He tried jumping high in the air. He tried getting a running start before he jumped. But no matter what he tried, the fox could not reach the grapes. As he angrily walked away, the fox muttered, "They were probably sour anyway!"

Moral: A person (or fox) sometimes pretends that he or she does not want something that cannot be had.

3. **This passage is which genre, or type of literature?**

   - (F) poetry
   - (G) biography
   - (H) nonfiction
   - (J) fable

4. **What clues in the story helped you decide what genre it is?**

   _____

   _____

   _____

   _____

   _____

My Backpack

My backpack's so heavy
It must weigh a ton.
With thousands of books—
My work's never done.

My arms are so sore
I can't lift a pen.
My breath is so short
I need oxygen.

When I stoop over,
It makes me fall down.
I think I'll just stay here
All squashed on the ground.

5. **This passage is which genre, or type, of literature?**

   - (A) nonfiction
   - (B) poetry
   - (C) biography
   - (D) fable

6. **What clues in the passage helped you decide what genre it is?**

   _____

   _____

   _____

   _____

   _____

   _____

STOP

English Language Arts
2.0

Responding to Literature
Reading and Comprehension

DIRECTIONS: Read the passage and answer the questions that follow.

The Un-Birthday

In my family, we don't celebrate birthdays—at least not like most families. My friends say I have an "un-birthday."

The tradition started with my grandmother. She and grandfather grew up in Poland. They escaped before World War II and made their way to America. When they got here, they were so grateful that they decided to share what they had with others. On their birthdays, they gave each other just one small gift. Then, they each bought a gift for someone who needed it more than they did.

As the years passed and the family grew, the tradition continued. On my last birthday, I got a backpack for school. We had a little party with cake and all of that. Then, we headed off to the Lionel School for disabled kids. Some of the children are in electric wheelchairs, and only a few can walk. I picked this school because my friend has a sister there.

When we walked in with our arms full of gifts, the kids were really excited. Even though we gave them little things—like sticker books and puzzles—all the presents were wrapped and had bows.

I gave Maggie, my friend's sister, a floppy, stuffed animal. Maggie can't talk, but she hugged her stuffed animal and looked at me, so I knew she was grateful.

I don't get as much stuff as my friends, but it's okay, even though I want a new skateboard. Seeing Maggie and the others receive their gifts was a lot better than getting a bunch of presents myself.

1. **How do you think the narrator feels about this unusual family tradition?**

_____

_____

_____

_____

2. **How does the narrator know that Maggie liked her gift?**

_____

_____

_____

3. **Why does the narrator call this family tradition an "un-birthday"?**

_____

_____

_____

4. **Would the narrator agree with the saying, "It is better to give than to receive"? Explain your answer.**

_____

_____

_____

_____

STOP

English Language Arts

| 3.0 |

Identifying Textual Features
Reading and Comprehension

DIRECTIONS: Read the passage and answer the questions that follow.

Kelp Forests

Both rain forests and kelp forests are important to our ecology. They keep animals safe by providing animal homes. Rain forests keep land animals safe, while kelp forests keep sea creatures safe.

Like rain forests, kelp forests are homes for many types of animals. Crab, eel, lobster, and seahorses are just a few of the sea creatures that live in sea kelp. In California alone, kelp forests are home to more than 770 animal species. A sandy ocean bottom can make a home for some creatures, but a kelp forest can make a home for thousands more. Why? The animals can live on the many kinds of kelp surfaces—rocky and leafy ones, for example.

Like a rain forest, a kelp forest has layers. You will find three main layers in a kelp forest. They are the canopy, middle, and floor layers. The canopy is at the top, and the floor is at the bottom.

You will find different sea creatures and plants at different levels. Herring and mackerel like to swim through the canopy. Sea slugs and snails feast on sea mats they find in the canopy.

Sea urchins look for food in the middle layer. Red seaweeds are often found in this layer of kelp forest as well, though they might be found at other levels.

Sea anemones, crabs, and lobsters live on the floor level. Older blue-rayed limpets feast here, too.

Like a rain forest, a kelp forest is a complex habitat for many sea creatures. It keeps them safe from predators and from people. To keep kelp forests an important part of our ecology, we must protect them from pollution and destruction.

1. How many paragraphs are in this passage?

- (A) 4
- (B) 5
- (C) 6
- (D) 7

2. Which sentence below describes the main idea of this passage?

- (F) A kelp forest has three levels.
- (G) Like rain forests, kelp forests help our ecology by providing homes for many animals.
- (H) Many sea creatures live in kelp forests and rain forests.
- (J) Kelp forests are like rain forests.

3. Which sentence is the topic sentence for paragraph 3?

- (A) sentence 1
- (B) sentence 2
- (C) sentence 3
- (D) sentence 4

4. Which sentence is the concluding sentence for the passage?

- (F) A kelp forest has layers.
- (G) To keep kelp forests an important part of our ecology, we must protect them from pollution and destruction.
- (H) Sea urchins look for food in the middle layer.
- (J) They are the canopy, middle, and floor layers.

STOP

English Language Arts

| 3.0 |

Evaluating Information
Reading and Comprehension

DIRECTIONS: Read the passage and answer the questions that follow.

The North Star

The North Star is one of the most famous stars. Its star name is *Polaris.* It is called the *North Star,* because it shines almost directly over the North Pole. If you are at the North Pole, the North Star is overhead. As you travel farther south, the star seems lower in the sky. Only people in the Northern Hemisphere can see the North Star.

Because the North Star is always in the same spot in the sky, it has been used for years to give direction to people at night. Sailors used the North Star to navigate through the oceans.

Polaris, like all stars, is always moving. Thousands of years from now, another star will get to be the North Star. Vega was the North Star thousands of years before it moved out of position and Polaris became the North Star.

1. **The North Star might be one of the most famous stars because _____ .**
   - (A) it is near the North Pole
   - (B) it is always moving
   - (C) it is always in the same spot in the sky
   - (D) it is difficult to find in the sky

2. **Another star will someday get to be the North Star because _____ .**
   - (F) stars are always moving
   - (G) there are many stars in the sky
   - (H) Earth will turn to the South Pole
   - (J) scientists rename it every 50 years

3. **The name *Polaris* most likely comes from which name?**
   - (A) polecat
   - (B) polar bear
   - (C) Poland
   - (D) North Pole

4. **Only people in the _____ Hemisphere can see the North Star.**
   - (F) Eastern
   - (G) Western
   - (H) Northern
   - (J) Southern

STOP

English Language Arts

| 3.0 |

Determining Meaning Using Content
Reading and Comprehension

DIRECTIONS: Read the passage and answer the questions that follow.

Snakes

How much do you know about snakes? Read these snake facts and find out.

- A snake skeleton has numerous ribs. A large snake may have as many as 400 pairs!
- Most snakes have poor eyesight. They track other animals by sensing their body heat.
- Snakes can't blink! They sleep with their eyes open.
- Although all snakes have teeth, very few of them—only the venomous ones—have fangs.
- Many snakes are very docile and unlikely to bite people.
- Pet snakes recognize their owners by smell. They flick their tongues in the air to detect smells.
- Snakes have special ways of hearing. Sound vibrations in the ground pass through their bellies to receptors in their spines. Airborne sounds pass through snakes' lungs to receptors in their skin.

1. *Numerous* means about the same as
   _____ .
   - (A) number
   - (B) many
   - (C) few
   - (D) special

2. In this passage, *poor* means the opposite of _____ .
   - (F) rich
   - (G) good
   - (H) happy
   - (J) broke

3. What does *track* mean as it is used in this passage?
   - (A) the rails on which a train moves
   - (B) a sport that includes running, jumping, and throwing
   - (C) to follow the footprints of
   - (D) to find and follow

4. What does the word *venomous* mean as it is used in this passage?
   - (F) vicious
   - (G) sharp
   - (H) poisonous
   - (J) huge

5. Which word means the opposite of *docile*?
   - (A) vicious
   - (B) shy
   - (C) gentle
   - (D) active

6. Which word means the same as *detect*?
   - (F) enjoy
   - (G) arrest
   - (H) find
   - (J) hide

7. A receptor _____ something.
   - (A) throws
   - (B) takes in
   - (C) gives
   - (D) sees

8. Airborne sounds are _____ .
   - (F) carried through the air
   - (G) carried through the earth
   - (H) always made by wind
   - (J) louder than other sounds

STOP

English Language Arts

| 1.0–3.0 |

For pages 9–17

Mini-Test 1

Reading and Comprehension

DIRECTIONS: Read the story, and then answer the questions.

Waterland

"Hurray!" cried Meghan. "Today is the day we're going to Waterland!" It was a hot July day, and Meghan's mom was taking her to cool off on the water slides. Meghan's new friend, Jake, was going, too.

Just then, Meghan's mom came out of her bedroom. She did not look very happy. "What's the matter, Mom? Are you afraid to get wet?" Meghan teased. "I'll bet you'll melt, just like the Wicked Witch of the West!"

Mrs. Millett didn't laugh at the joke. Instead, she told the kids that she wasn't feeling well. She was too tired to drive to the water park.

Meghan and Jake were disappointed. "My mom has chronic fatigue syndrome," Meghan explained. "Her illness makes her really tired. She's still a great mom."

"Thank you, dear," said Mrs. Millett. "I'm too tired to drive, but I have an idea. You can make your own Waterland and I'll rest in the lawn chair."

Meghan and Jake set up three different sprinklers. They dragged the play slide over to the wading pool and aimed the sprinkler on the slide. Meghan and Jake got soaking wet. Mrs. Millett sat in a lawn chair and rested. The kids played all day.

"Thank you for being so understanding," Meghan's mom said. "Now I feel better, but I'm really hot! There's only one cure for that." She stood under the sprinkler with all her clothes on. She was drenched from head to toe.

Meghan laughed and said, "Now you have chronic wet syndrome." Mrs. Millett rewarded her daughter with a big, wet hug. It turned out to be a wonderful day after all in the backyard waterland.

1. This passage is an example of which genre, or type of literature?

- (A) biography
- (B) fable
- (C) fiction
- (D) nonfiction

2. Which sentence best tells the main idea of this story?

- (F) Meghan's mom has chronic fatigue syndrome.
- (G) Jake and Meghan miss out on Waterland, but they make their own water park and have fun anyway.
- (H) Jake and Meghan cannot go to Waterland.
- (J) Sprinklers make a great backyard water park.

3. How do you think Mrs. Millett feels about not being able to take the kids to Waterland?

- (A) She's glad that she won't have to spend her whole day with kids.
- (B) She feels sorry for herself and is glad she got out of it.
- (C) She's disappointed that she can't take them.
- (D) She's hurt and confused.

4. In this story, *fatigue* means the same as _____ .

- (F) to be excited
- (G) to be tired
- (H) to be sad
- (J) to be sick

STOP

English Language Arts

| 4.0 |

Using Words Correctly
Writing

DIRECTIONS: Choose the word that means the same or about the same as the underlined word.

1. <u>high</u> fence

- (A) tall
- (B) happy
- (C) long
- (D) wide

2. <u>paste</u> the paper

- (F) fold
- (G) attach
- (H) patch
- (J) glue

3. If something is moving <u>swiftly</u>, it is moving _____ .

- (A) slowly
- (B) smoothly
- (C) quickly
- (D) on the land

4. <u>Shallow</u> means _____ .

- (F) not intelligent
- (G) deep
- (H) not deep
- (J) able to swim

DIRECTIONS: Choose the meaning for each underlined word.

5. The wings of the butterflies were <u>fluttering</u> in the breeze.

Fluttering means _____ .

- (A) waving
- (B) colorful
- (C) lovely
- (D) flashing

6. Gazelles and impalas are <u>prey</u> to the cheetah.

Prey means _____ .

- (F) food
- (G) friends
- (H) similar
- (J) predators

7. David gave his sister a <u>smirk</u>.

Smirk means _____ .

- (A) friendly smile
- (B) scar
- (C) smug expression
- (D) facemask

DIRECTIONS: Choose the word that means the opposite of the underlined word.

8. <u>valuable</u> painting

- (F) strange
- (G) expensive
- (H) worthless
- (J) humorous

9. <u>loose</u> tie

- (A) tight
- (B) lost
- (C) plain
- (D) ill fitting

10. <u>narrow</u> ledge

- (F) thin
- (G) cement
- (H) skinny
- (J) wide

STOP

Name _____ Date _____

English Language Arts

Varying
Sentence Structure
Writing

DIRECTIONS: Write **S** before each line that is a simple sentence or a complete thought. Write **F** before each line that is a sentence fragment or incomplete thought.

1. _____ **You should know better.**

2. _____ **Walking faster all the time.**

3. _____ **Wait outside.**

4. _____ **Caught the ball and threw it to second base.**

5. _____ **Every house in town.**

6. _____ **The dog jumped over the fence.**

7. _____ **They will arrive soon.**

8. _____ **Can you close the window?**

9. _____ **A few people in this club.**

10. _____ **He can read well.**

DIRECTIONS: Choose the answer that best combines the sentences.

11. **Pedro finished his homework.**
    Pedro went to bed.

    Ⓐ Pedro finished his homework or went to bed.

    Ⓑ Pedro finished his homework and then went to bed.

    Ⓒ Pedro finished his homework because he went to bed.

    Ⓓ Going to bed, Pedro finished his homework

12. **The truck brought the furniture to our house. The truck was large.**

    Ⓕ The large truck, which brought the furniture to our house.

    Ⓖ The truck was large that brought the furniture to our house.

    Ⓗ The truck brought the furniture to our house, and was large.

    Ⓙ The large truck brought the furniture to our house.

DIRECTIONS: A **compound sentence** is made up of two complete thoughts, or simple sentences, that are joined by a conjunction. Use the conjunctions *and, or,* or *but* after the comma to complete each sentence.

13. **Sasha flew to Chicago, _____ she took a train to Milwaukee.**

14. **I can go to the game, _____ I have to be home by ten.**

15. **Finish your homework, _____ you won't be allowed to play outside.**

16. **Some athletes are paid well, _____ others do not make much money.**

17. **His favorite food is pizza, _____ his favorite drink is lemonade.**

18. **Miss Steiner is known as a poet, _____ she can also sing and dance.**

19. **You can spend your money on ice cream, _____ you can save your money to buy a toy.**

STOP

English Language Arts

4.0/5.0

Identifying Types of Sentences
Writing

DIRECTIONS: Below are several sentences. Identify what type of sentence each one is by writing **DE** for declarative, **IN** for interrogative, **IM** for imperative, and **EX** for exclamatory.

Examples:

A **declarative** sentence makes a statement and has a period at the end.
> *Ben walked home from school with Jaime.*

An **interrogative** sentence asks a question and ends with a question mark.
> *Will you feed the fish today?*

And **exclamatory** sentence shows excitement or emotion and ends with an exclamation mark.
> *Hey! Stop hitting me!*

An **imperative** sentence expresses a command or request and ends with a period.
> *Come to the principal's office now.*

_____ 1. He quickly looked around to see if anyone was watching him.

_____ 2. He fled toward the barn.

_____ 3. Can you keep a secret?

_____ 4. Not a chance!

_____ 5. Do not stop reading until you reach the end of this story.

_____ 6. Jack stood on the deck of the ship.

_____ 7. Get back in your room.

_____ 8. What kind of cat do you have?

_____ 9. What a joke!

_____ 10. They looked for a place to hide their treasure.

_____ 11. Where do you want to eat lunch?

_____ 12. Don't touch that picture.

_____ 13. I think I forgot my lunch at home.

_____ 14. Mom is going to be mad at me!

_____ 15. What are you going to do?

_____ 16. Clean up that mess right now.

STOP

English Language Arts

| 5.0 |

Using an Organizational Structure
Writing

DIRECTIONS: Kyle was working on a report for his class. He could write about any animal he chose. Kyle loved owls and decided to make them the topic of his report. Before he started writing, he developed the following outline. Study the outline and answer the questions that follow.

Owls

I. _____

    A. Great Horned Owl

    B. Snowy Owl

    C. Barn Owl

II. **Body Characteristics**

    A. Size

    B. Body Covering

    C. _____

    D. Eyes, Talons, and Beaks

III. **Eating Habits**

    A. Mice

    B. Other Small Rodents

1. **Which of the following fits best in the blank next to I.?**

    (A) Owl Migration

    (B) Owl Habitats

    (C) Types of Owls

    (D) Owl Eating Habits

2. **Which of the following fits best in the blank next to C.?**

    (F) Feather Variations

    (G) Grasses and Leaves

    (H) Trees

    (J) Nocturnal

3. **Explain how the organization of the outline will help Kyle as he writes his report.**

_____

_____

_____

_____

_____

_____

_____

_____

STOP

English Language Arts

| 5.0 |

Writing With Details
Writing

DIRECTIONS: This is the beginning of a story. Read it and use your own ideas to help you finish the story.

> It was finally getting cooler. After a blazing, hot day, the sun had finally gone down. Hannah still couldn't believe their car had broken down. She also couldn't believe her father had decided to walk three miles through the desert for help. The map showed a town up ahead, but they hadn't seen any cars go by for over an hour. She was alone with her mother and her sister, Abigail.

1. **What problem does Hannah's family have?**

_____

_____

_____

_____

2. **Describe two ways that this story might turn out.**

_____

_____

_____

_____

_____

_____

_____

_____

3. **What are some of the sounds, sights, and feelings that Hannah's family might have experienced?**

_____

_____

_____

_____

_____

_____

_____

_____

_____

_____

_____

_____

_____

4. **Use the details from your answers to questions 1–3 to write the ending to the story on a separate piece of paper.**

STOP

English Language Arts

| 5.0 |

Writing a Persuasive Essay
Writing

DIRECTIONS: Read the paragraph about a book one student really liked. Then, answer each question below.

> I really liked the book *The Wizard of Oz* and think others will like it, too. It was very exciting, especially the part where Dorothy went to the Wicked Witch's castle and made the Witch melt. I also liked the way the characters worked together to solve their problems. Finally, when Dorothy says, "There's no place like home," I thought about my home and the many wonderful things I have.

1. **Think of a book or movie you really liked. What is its title?**

   _____

   _____

2. **Why do you think others should read or watch it?**

   _____

   _____

   _____

   _____

   _____

3. **What are some specific parts of the book or movie that you think others would enjoy?**

   _____

   _____

   _____

   _____

   _____

   _____

4. **Now, write a few paragraphs using the information from questions 2 and 3 to convince others to read this book or watch the movie. Explain why you liked this book or movie and include examples from the book or movie to support your reasons. Be sure to use as many details as possible to persuade readers to read or watch it.**

   _____

   _____

   _____

   _____

   _____

   _____

   _____

   _____

   _____

   _____

   _____

   _____

   _____

   _____

STOP

English Language Arts

5.0

Writing a Narrative Procedure
Writing

DIRECTIONS: Read the paragraph below about how to plant a seed. Then, think of something you know how to do well. Write a narrative procedure that explains how to do it. Use paragraphs and words such as *first, next, then, finally,* and *last.*

> I found out how to plant a seed and make it grow. First, I found a spot where the plant would get the right amount of sunshine. Next, I dug a hole, put the seed into the soil, and then covered the seed with soil. Then, I watered the seed. After a couple weeks, it began to grow into a beautiful plant.

Clue

A **narrative procedure** explains how to do something. It uses clear steps that are easy to follow.

_____

_____

_____

_____

_____

_____

_____

_____

_____

_____

_____

_____

_____

_____

STOP

English Language Arts

| 6.0 |

Spelling
Writing

DIRECTIONS: Find the word that is spelled correctly and fits best in the blank.

1. Please _____ your work.

- (A) revew
- (B) reeview
- (C) review
- (D) raview

2. He is my best _____ .

- (F) frind
- (G) frend
- (H) friend
- (J) freind

3. We can _____ the gymnasium.

- (A) decarate
- (B) decorait
- (C) decorrate
- (D) decorate

4. The store is in a good _____ .

- (F) locashun
- (G) locashin
- (H) locatin
- (J) location

5. Students were _____ for bravery.

- (A) honored
- (B) honord
- (C) honered
- (D) honard

6. The train _____ arrived.

- (F) finaly
- (G) finnalie
- (H) finely
- (J) finally

DIRECTIONS: Read each word. Choose the word that has a spelling error.

7.
- (A) service
- (B) fountain
- (C) suceed
- (D) complete

8.
- (F) recieve
- (G) observe
- (H) information
- (J) appear

9.
- (A) jury
- (B) knuckle
- (C) illegal
- (D) pollite

10.
- (F) wildernes
- (G) structure
- (H) republic
- (J) misunderstood

11.
- (A) contact
- (B) position
- (C) prettier
- (D) allready

STOP

English Language Arts

6.0

Capitalization and Punctuation
Writing

DIRECTIONS: Rewrite the sentences below using the correct capitalization and punctuation.

1. **tyson began singing the star-spangled banner**

   _____

   _____

   _____

   _____

2. **joe read an article about canadian geese in a magazine**

   _____

   _____

   _____

   _____

3. **we sold school supplies to help raise money for the red cross**

   _____

   _____

   _____

   _____

4. **i'm really glad you are here abby said**

   _____

   _____

   _____

   _____

DIRECTIONS: Choose the sentence that shows correct punctuation and capitalization.

5. (A) Tell Mrs Jensen I called.

   (B) Miss. Richards will be late.

   (C) Our coach is Mr. Wannamaker

   (D) Dr. Cullin was here earlier.

6. (F) Will you please take the garbage out

   (G) Dont let Rachel forget her chores.

   (H) She has been reading *Charlotte's Web* all afternoon.

   (J) This house looks like a pigsty

7. (A) "I suggest you go the library to do research," Mom said.

   (B) "The *world book encyclopedia* is a good place to look."

   (C) "I will help you look in *National Geographic* when you get home.

   (D) Your report will be perfect when you're done," Mom insisted.

8. (F) Joel hurt his wrist, yesterday while playing hockey.

   (G) However, he scored three goals in the process.

   (H) He will be the champion of patterson Ice Center.

   (J) Perhaps they will loan him the stanley cup

STOP

English Language Arts

6.0

Using Figurative Language
Writing

DIRECTIONS: Fill in the blanks to complete the similes from the poem.

Polar Bears

With fur like a snowstorm
And eyes like the night,
Two giant old bears
Sure gave me a fright.

They came up behind me
As quiet as mice,
And tapped on my shoulder.
Their paws were like ice.

As high as a kite,
I jumped in the air,
And turned round to see
Those bears standing there.

"We're sorry we scared you,"
The bears said so cool.
"We just came to ask you
To fill up our pool!"

Clue

Figurative language is language used for descriptive effect. This poem uses **similes**. Similes use *like* or *as* to compare things that may seem unlike each other.

1. **fur like** _____

2. **eyes like** _____

3. **as quiet as** _____

4. **paws like** _____

5. **as high as a** _____

DIRECTIONS: Write your own similes using these words as a guide. Compare two things by using the words *like* or *as*.

6. **a lunch** *as* _____ *as*

_____

7. **a friend** *like* **a** _____

8. **a coat** *as* _____ *as*

_____

9. **a winter day** *like* **a** _____

10. **with** _____ *like* **sunshine**

STOP

English Language Arts

| 4.0–6.0 |

For pages 19–28

Mini-Test 2

Writing

---

1. <u>Infect</u> means _____ .

   Ⓐ to act

   Ⓑ to cheer up

   Ⓒ to spread disease

   Ⓓ to discover

2. I <u>sprinted</u> to the finish line.

   Sprinted means _____ .

   Ⓕ skipped

   Ⓖ crawled

   Ⓗ ran very quickly

   Ⓙ tripped

3. **Read the following sentence. What type of sentence is it?**

   What is your favorite food?

   Ⓐ declarative

   Ⓑ imperative

   Ⓒ exclamatory

   Ⓓ interrogative

4. **Which of the following types of writing would not be a persuasive essay?**

   Ⓕ a review of your favorite book that describes why others should read it

   Ⓖ a letter to the editor explaining why your community should have a new park

   Ⓗ a story about your family's vacation

   Ⓙ a letter to your parents stating the reasons you should get an increase in your allowance

5. **Which answer has a spelling error?**

   Ⓐ reproduce

   Ⓑ usualy

   Ⓒ interest

   Ⓓ happily

6. **Combine the group of sentences into one sentence.**

   Horses can walk. They can trot. They can gallop.

   _____

   _____

DIRECTIONS: Choose the answer that shows correct punctuation and capitalization.

7. Ⓐ The house is very large

   Ⓑ what did you say?

   Ⓒ The Tennis courts are full.

   Ⓓ Kaylie put our names on the list.

8. Ⓕ Tell Mrs Jensen I called.

   Ⓖ Miss. Richards will be late.

   Ⓗ Our coach is Mr. Slate.

   Ⓙ Did you remember your homework assignment

DIRECTIONS: Choose the answer that best combines the sentences.

9. **Arnie found a ball.**
   The ball was red.
   He found it on the way to school.

   Ⓐ Finding a red ball, Arnie was on his way to school.

   Ⓑ Arnie found a red ball on the way to school.

   Ⓒ Arnie found a ball on the way to school that was red.

   Ⓓ The red ball that Arnie found on the way to school.

English Language Arts

7.0

Analyzing Informational Reports
Research

DIRECTIONS: Read the passage and answer the questions that follow.

> Perhaps you have heard that many types of bats have very small eyes and do not see well. Still, as they swoop through the night, they do not bump into objects and are able to find food, even though they can't see their prey. How is this possible? Echolocation!
>
> You might recognize the beginning of the word *echolocation* as *echo*, and you might recognize the last part of the word as *location*. This gives you clues about how echolocation works. The bat sends out sounds. The sounds bounce off objects and return to the bat. Echolocation not only tells the bat that objects are nearby, it also tells the bat just how far away the objects are.
>
> Bats are not the only creatures that use echolocation. Porpoises and some types of whales and birds use it as well. It is a very effective tool for the animals that use it.

1. **What is the main idea of this passage?**

   _____

   _____

   _____

   _____

   _____

2. **Why do you think the writer chose to show how the word *echolocation* can be broken into *echo* and *location*?**

   _____

   _____

   _____

   _____

   _____

3. **Based on this passage, what are two questions about bats that you would like to have answered?**

   _____

   _____

   _____

   _____

4. **Name some resources that you could use to find the answers to the questions you wrote in question 3.**

   _____

   _____

   _____

   _____

   _____

STOP

English Language Arts

8.0

Using a Dictionary
Research

Clue

Dictionaries have **guide words** that appear at the top corners of each page. Guide words identify the first and last words that appear on each page. Also, dictionary entries can tell you more than just the meaning of a word. They can also help you say a word correctly and tell you if a word is a noun, verb, adjective, adverb, or pronoun.

DIRECTIONS: Use the dictionary entries to answer questions 1–3.

save [sāv] *v.* **1.** to rescue from harm or danger **2.** to keep in a safe condition **3.** to set aside for future use; store **4.** to avoid

saving [sā´vĭng] *n.* **1.** rescuing from harm or danger **2.** avoiding excess spending; economy **3.** something saved

savory [sā´və-rē] *adj.* **1.** appealing to the taste or smell **2.** salty to the taste

1. **The *a* in the word *saving* sounds most like the word _____ .**
   - Ⓐ pat
   - Ⓑ ape
   - Ⓒ heated
   - Ⓓ naughty

2. **Which sentence uses *save* in the same way as definition number 3?**
   - Ⓕ Firefighters save lives.
   - Ⓖ She saves half of all she earns.
   - Ⓗ Going by jet saves eight hours of driving.
   - Ⓙ The life jacket saved the boy from drowning.

3. **Which sentence uses *savory* in the same way as definition number 2?**
   - Ⓐ The savory stew made me thirsty.
   - Ⓑ The savory bank opened an account.
   - Ⓒ This flower has a savory scent.
   - Ⓓ The savory dog rescued me.

DIRECTIONS: Choose the best answer.

4. **Look at the guide words. Which word would be found on this page of the dictionary?**
   - Ⓕ brute
   - Ⓖ broken
   - Ⓗ burn
   - Ⓙ brake

guide words
branch–brown

5. **Which word would be found on this page of the dictionary?**
   - Ⓐ puppy
   - Ⓑ pet
   - Ⓒ protect
   - Ⓓ punish

guide words
prize–pump

6. **Which word would be found on this page of the dictionary?**
   - Ⓕ stress
   - Ⓖ strong
   - Ⓗ stick
   - Ⓙ strum

guide words
strawberry–stroll

7. **Which word would be found on this page of the dictionary?**
   - Ⓐ arctic
   - Ⓑ ape
   - Ⓒ aster
   - Ⓓ assure

guide words
apple–assume

English Language Arts

8.0

Using Resources
Research

DIRECTIONS: Use the picture of encyclopedias to answer questions 1–4.

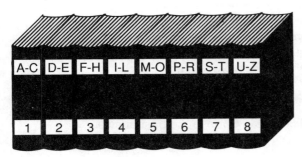

1. In which volume would you find information about different types of flags?

  Ⓐ volume 2
  Ⓑ volume 3
  Ⓒ volume 5
  Ⓓ volume 7

2. Which of the following topics would be found in volume 5?

  Ⓕ information about the Moon
  Ⓖ how to knit
  Ⓗ world climate regions
  Ⓙ the life of John F. Kennedy

3. Where would you find an article about Thomas Jefferson?

  Ⓐ volume 7
  Ⓑ volume 4
  Ⓒ volume 1
  Ⓓ volume 3

4. Which of the following topics would be found in volume 1?

  Ⓕ bears
  Ⓖ democracy
  Ⓗ North America
  Ⓙ Underground Railroad

DIRECTIONS: Study this entry from an electronic card catalog. Use it to answer questions 5–7.

> **AUTHOR:** Lyons, Nick
> **TITLE:** Confessions of a fly-fishing addict/Nick Lyons.
> **PUBLISHER:** New York : Simon & Schuster, c1989
> **DESCRIPT:** 200 p. : 22 cm
> **SUBJECTS:** Fly fishing
> **ADD TITLE:** Confessions of a fly-fishing addict
> **ISBN:** 067168379
> **CALL NUMBER:** 799.12 Lyo : 9/89

5. What is the call number for this book?

  Ⓐ 799.12
  Ⓑ 1989
  Ⓒ 200
  Ⓓ 067168379

6. Choose the label for the shelf on which you would look for this book.

  Ⓕ 500–600
  Ⓖ 600–700
  Ⓗ 700–800
  Ⓙ 800–900

7. In what year was this book published?

  Ⓐ 2000
  Ⓑ 1989
  Ⓒ 1799
  Ⓓ 2005

8. If a book's call number is 234.48, on which shelf in the library would you find it?

  Ⓕ 800–890
  Ⓖ 540–599
  Ⓗ 220–285
  Ⓙ 200–232

STOP

English Language Arts

7.0–8.0

For pages 30–32

Mini-Test 3

Research

DIRECTIONS: Use the dictionary entry to answer questions 1 and 2.

beam [bēm] *n.* **1.** a squared-off log used to support a building **2.** a ray of light **3.** the wooden roller in a loom *v.* **1.** to shine **2.** to smile broadly

1. **Which sentence uses the word *beam* in the same way as the first definition of the noun?**
   - (A) The beam held up the plaster ceiling.
   - (B) The beam of sunlight warmed the room.
   - (C) She moved the beam before she added a row of wool.
   - (D) The bright stars beam in the night sky.

2. **Which sentence uses the word *beam* in the same way as the third definition of the noun?**
   - (F) The ceiling beam had fallen into the room.
   - (G) She moved the beam before she added a row of wool.
   - (H) She beamed her approval.
   - (J) The beam of sunlight came through the tree.

DIRECTIONS: Choose the best answer.

3. **Look at these guide words. Which word would be found on this page of a dictionary?**
   - (A) frail
   - (B) failure
   - (C) fracture
   - (D) flunk

guide words
fourth–fragile

DIRECTIONS: Use the picture of encyclopedias to answer questions 4 and 5.

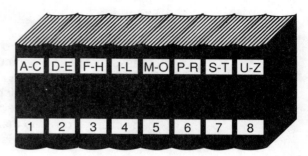

4. **In which volume would you find information about whales?**
   - (F) volume 2
   - (G) volume 3
   - (H) volume 5
   - (J) volume 8

5. **Which of the following topics would be found in volume 2?**
   - (A) information about bats
   - (B) the water cycle
   - (C) information about stars
   - (D) the life of Frederick Douglass

6. **If a book's call number is 683.2, on which shelf would you find it?**
   - (F) 220–285
   - (G) 540–599
   - (H) 600–685
   - (J) 686–734

7. **The following call numbers appear on different books. Which one would you find on shelf 540–599?**
   - (A) 589.88
   - (B) 539.1
   - (C) 501.35
   - (D) 600.5

STOP

English Language Arts

9.0

Identifying Cultural Language Use
Cultural and Social Language Use

Example:

You may have heard people use certain words or phrases that have a particular meaning in the area or culture in which you live. Someone who is not from your area or culture may not understand what those words or phrases mean. These phrases or sayings are called **colloquialisms.** Many cultures develop their own colloquialisms. Here is an example of one that is used in the United States:

"Hold your horses" means *to be patient* or *slow down.*

DIRECTIONS: Below are some colloquialisms used in the United States. Match the phrases in Column A with their meanings in Column B.

Column A

_____ 1. bury the hatchet

_____ 2. bite the bullet

_____ 3. forty winks

_____ 4. knee-high to a grasshopper

_____ 5. squirrel away

_____ 6. strike while the iron is hot

_____ 7. worn to a frazzle

_____ 8. kick the bucket

Column B

a. to do something difficult

b. to die

c. to take a nap

d. to do something immediately

e. to be very tired

f. to make peace with someone

g. to store up for future use

h. to be very young

DIRECTIONS: Below are some colloquialisms used in Australia. Try to match the phrases in Column A with their meanings in Column B.

Column A

_____ 9. ankle biter

_____ 10. it's gone walkabout

_____ 11. mad as a cut snake

_____ 12. up a gum tree

Column B

a. to be in a rage

b. a small child

c. to be stranded

d. to have lost something

English Language Arts

11.0

Sharing a Book Review
Cultural and Social Language Use

DIRECTIONS: In your class at school, you are part of a reading community. The other students in your class all read books. Each one of you likes and dislikes different things about the books you read. Ask a friend in your class to do this activity with you. Pick out a book that you can both read at the same time. Or use a book that you have read together in class. After you are done reading the book, answer the following questions. Use an extra sheet of paper to record your answers if needed.

1. **What is the title of the book?** _____

2. **What genre, or type of literature, is the book?** _____

3. **Describe what the book is about. Include any main characters and the plot or problem.**

   _____

   _____

   _____

4. **What was your favorite part in the book? Why was it your favorite?**

   _____

   _____

   _____

5. **What was your least favorite part in the book? Why was it your least favorite?**

   _____

   _____

   _____

6. **Do you think the author did a good job writing the book? If so, why? If not, what would you change about the book?**

   _____

   _____

   _____

   _____

7. **Use your answers to the above questions to help you develop a review of the book. When you are done, share your book review with your friend. Compare your answers. Did you like or dislike the same parts? Why or why not? Did you agree about how well the author did in writing the book? Why or why not?**

STOP

English Language Arts

12.0

Writing a
Personal Narrative
Cultural and Social Language Use

DIRECTIONS: Write about something that happened to you while you were on vacation. Include descriptions of places and people, interesting details, and feelings you had during your experience.

Clue

A **personal narrative** is a true story that is based on a person's experiences. It should have a clear beginning, middle, and end.

STOP

English Language Arts

| 9.0–12.0 |

For pages 34–36

Mini-Test 4

Cultural and Social Language Use

DIRECTIONS: Choose the best answer.

1. The phrase "raining cats and dogs" means
   _____ .
   - (A) it is barely raining
   - (B) it is raining very heavily
   - (C) it is raining and snowing both
   - (D) problems are plentiful

2. To "bury the hatchet" means to _____ .
   - (F) finish a project
   - (G) die
   - (H) make peace
   - (J) stop working

3. What does someone want you to do if they tell you to "hold your horses"?
   - (A) be patient
   - (B) hurry up
   - (C) be careful
   - (D) get excited

4. A person who is "wet behind the ears" is
   _____ .
   - (F) sweaty
   - (G) exhausted
   - (H) prepared
   - (J) young or inexperienced

5. Which of the following phrases means "to die"?
   - (A) kick the bucket
   - (B) hang up your boots
   - (C) cross over to the other side
   - (D) all of the above

DIRECTIONS: Describe what it was like when you did something for the first time. Some ideas include playing a new sport, learning how to play an instrument, acting in a play, or starting a new hobby. Include details or feelings you had during this experience.

6. _____

_____

_____

_____

_____

_____

_____

_____

_____

_____

_____

_____

_____

_____

_____

_____

_____

_____

_____

_____

_____

_____

STOP

How Am I Doing?

Mini-Test 1

Page 18

Number Correct

4 answers correct	**Great Job!** Move on to the section test on page 40.
3 answers correct	**You're almost there!** But you still need a little practice. Review practice pages 9–17 before moving on to the section test on page 40.
0–2 answers correct	**Oops!** Time to review what you have learned and try again. Review the practice section on pages 9–17. Then, retake the test on page 18. Now, move on to the section test on page 40.

Mini-Test 2

Page 29

Number Correct

8–9 answers correct	**Awesome!** Move on to the section test on page 40.
4–7 answers correct	**You're almost there!** But you still need a little practice. Review practice pages 19–28 before moving on to the section test on page 40.
0–3 answers correct	**Oops!** Time to review what you have learned and try again. Review the practice section on pages 19–28. Then, retake the test on page 29. Now, move on to the section test on page 40.

Mini-Test 3

Page 33

Number Correct

7 answers correct	**Great Job!** Move on to the section test on page 40.
5–6 answers correct	**You're almost there!** But you still need a little practice. Review practice pages 30–32 before moving on to the section test on page 40.
0–4 answers correct	**Oops!** Time to review what you have learned and try again. Review the practice section on pages 30–32. Then, retake the test on page 33. Now, move on to the section test on page 40.

How Am I Doing?

Mini-Test 4	6 answers correct	**Awesome!** Move on to the section test on page 40.
Page 37 **Number Correct**	4–5 answers correct	**You're almost there!** But you still need a little practice. Review practice pages 34–36 before moving on to the section test on page 40.
	0–3 answers correct	**Oops!** Time to review what you have learned and try again. Review the practice section on pages 34–36. Then, retake the test on page 37. Now, move on to the section test on page 40.

Name _____ Date _____

Final English Language Arts Test
for pages 9–37

DIRECTIONS: Read the passage, and then answer questions 1–3.

Helping the Mountain Gorilla

Mountain gorillas live in the rain forests in Rwanda, Uganda, and the Democratic Republic of the Congo. These large, beautiful animals are becoming very rare. They have lost much of their habitat as people move in and take over the gorillas' lands. Although there are strict laws protecting gorillas, poachers continue to hunt them.

Scientists observe gorillas to learn about their habits and needs. Then, scientists write about their findings in magazines. Concerned readers sometimes give money to help protect the mountain gorillas.

Many other people are working hard to protect the mountain gorillas. Park rangers patrol the rain forest and arrest poachers. Tourists bring much-needed money into the area, encouraging local residents to protect the gorillas, too.

1. **What is this passage mainly about?**
   - (A) mountain gorillas' family relationships
   - (B) scientists who study mountain gorillas
   - (C) ways that gorillas are being harmed and helped
   - (D) poachers and wars that threaten gorillas' survival

2. **Which words help you figure out the meaning of *habitat*?**
   - (F) "large, beautiful animals"
   - (G) "gorillas' lands"
   - (H) "the human population"
   - (J) "recent civil wars"

3. **The author's purpose for writing this passage is to _____ .**
   - (A) entertain readers
   - (B) inform readers about mountain gorillas
   - (C) motivate readers to visit Rwanda
   - (D) explain to readers where Africa is

4. **The author of the passage thinks that tourism _____ .**
   - (F) is very harmful to mountain gorillas
   - (G) is one cause of civil wars in Africa
   - (H) can be helpful to mountain gorillas
   - (J) is one cause of overpopulation in Africa

5. **This passage is an example of which genre of literature?**
   - (A) poetry
   - (B) biography
   - (C) nonfiction
   - (D) fable

DIRECTIONS: Choose the meaning for each underlined word.

6. <u>chilly</u> day
   - (F) long
   - (G) frozen
   - (H) cold
   - (J) unpleasant

7. We were <u>exhausted</u> after running. *Exhausted* means _____ .
   - (A) very tired
   - (B) refreshed
   - (C) excited
   - (D) wide awake

DIRECTIONS: Choose the word that means the opposite of the underlined word.

8. **<u>rough</u> board**
   - (F) large
   - (G) heavy
   - (H) smooth
   - (J) long

9. **<u>hilarious</u> movie**
   - (A) scary
   - (B) long
   - (C) sad
   - (D) confusing

DIRECTIONS: Choose the word that means the same, or about the same, as the underlined word.

10. **<u>irritated</u> teacher**
    - (F) excited
    - (G) helpful
    - (H) annoyed
    - (J) boring

11. **<u>baggy</u> pants**
    - (A) loose
    - (B) brown
    - (C) tight
    - (D) made of cotton

DIRECTIONS: Choose the word that is spelled correctly and best completes the sentence.

12. **Three _____ people lived in the city.**
    - (F) milion
    - (G) millun
    - (H) millione
    - (J) million

13. **Do you like _____ movies?**
    - (A) horrorr
    - (B) horor
    - (C) horror
    - (D) horrer

DIRECTIONS: Choose the line that has a punctuation error. If there is no error, choose "no mistakes."

14.
   - (F) The bus will pick us up
   - (G) at 830 a.m. sharp for
   - (H) the field trip to the zoo.
   - (J) no mistakes

15.
   - (A) Sara wanted to adopt
   - (B) another greyhound but
   - (C) she simply didn't have room.
   - (D) no mistakes

16.
   - (F) Clare, Andrea and I
   - (G) were next in line
   - (H) for the roller coaster.
   - (J) no mistakes

DIRECTIONS: Choose the answer that fits best in the blank and shows correct capitalization and punctuation.

17. **The new mall will open on _____ .**
    - (A) may 1 2007
    - (B) May 1, 2007
    - (C) may 1, 2007
    - (D) May, 1, 2007

18. **Do you think we should go swimming, _____**
    - (F) Sam?
    - (G) sam.
    - (H) sam!
    - (J) Sam.

GO

19. Which of the following sentences is an example of a declarative sentence?

- (A) What did you get for your birthday?
- (B) I can't believe it!
- (C) It was a very cold day.
- (D) Bring me the book that is on the counter.

20. Which of the following sentences is an example of an interrogative sentence?

- (F) You've got to be kidding!
- (G) What time is it?
- (H) Don't run out in the street.
- (J) Darcy went to the store.

21. Which of the following sentences is a fragment?

- (A) Her favorite color is blue.
- (B) She wears it every day.
- (C) While she sometimes wears pink.
- (D) She never wears the color green.

22. Which conjunction would fit best in the blank?

Turner studies hard for his tests, _____ he gets good grades.

- (F) but
- (G) and
- (H) for
- (J) or

DIRECTIONS: Choose the answer that best combines the sentences.

23. The room was filled with children.
The children were happy.

- (A) The room was filled with happy children.
- (B) The room was filled and the children were happy.
- (C) The children were happy who filled the room.
- (D) Filled with happy children was the room.

24. Look at these guide words from a dictionary page.

guide words
nothing–now

Which of the following words could be found on this page?

- (F) novel
- (G) nose
- (H) notepaper
- (J) nowhere

25. If a book's call number is 653.12, on which shelf would you find it at the library?

- (A) 500–600
- (B) 600–700
- (C) 700–800
- (D) 800–900

26. In an outline, which of these words would be the best heading for the other words?

- (F) People
- (G) Government
- (H) Climate
- (J) Bolivia

DIRECTIONS: Use the picture of encyclopedias to answer the question.

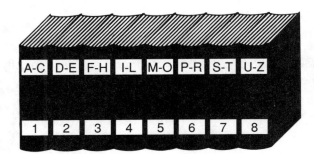

27. In which volume would you find information about different types of lizards?

- (A) volume 2
- (B) volume 4
- (C) volume 5
- (D) volume 7

Final English Language Arts Test
Answer Sheet

1 Ⓐ Ⓑ Ⓒ Ⓓ
2 Ⓕ Ⓖ Ⓗ Ⓙ
3 Ⓐ Ⓑ Ⓒ Ⓓ
4 Ⓕ Ⓖ Ⓗ Ⓙ
5 Ⓐ Ⓑ Ⓒ Ⓓ
6 Ⓕ Ⓖ Ⓗ Ⓙ
7 Ⓐ Ⓑ Ⓒ Ⓓ
8 Ⓕ Ⓖ Ⓗ Ⓙ
9 Ⓐ Ⓑ Ⓒ Ⓓ
10 Ⓕ Ⓖ Ⓗ Ⓙ

11 Ⓐ Ⓑ Ⓒ Ⓓ
12 Ⓕ Ⓖ Ⓗ Ⓙ
13 Ⓐ Ⓑ Ⓒ Ⓓ
14 Ⓕ Ⓖ Ⓗ Ⓙ
15 Ⓐ Ⓑ Ⓒ Ⓓ
16 Ⓕ Ⓖ Ⓗ Ⓙ
17 Ⓐ Ⓑ Ⓒ Ⓓ
18 Ⓕ Ⓖ Ⓗ Ⓙ
19 Ⓐ Ⓑ Ⓒ Ⓓ
20 Ⓕ Ⓖ Ⓗ Ⓙ

21 Ⓐ Ⓑ Ⓒ Ⓓ
22 Ⓕ Ⓖ Ⓗ Ⓙ
23 Ⓐ Ⓑ Ⓒ Ⓓ
24 Ⓕ Ⓖ Ⓗ Ⓙ
25 Ⓐ Ⓑ Ⓒ Ⓓ
26 Ⓕ Ⓖ Ⓗ Ⓙ
27 Ⓐ Ⓑ Ⓒ Ⓓ

Mathematics Standards

Standard 1—Number and Operations *(See pages 45–49.)*
  A. Understand numbers, ways of representing numbers, relationships among numbers, and number systems.
  B. Understand meanings of operations and how they relate to one another.
  C. Compute fluently and make reasonable estimates.

Standard 2—Algebra *(See pages 50–54.)*
  A. Understand patterns, relations, and functions.
  B. Represent and analyze mathematical situations and structures using algebraic symbols.
  C. Use mathematical models to represent and understand quantitative relationships.
  D. Analyze change in various contexts.

Standard 3—Geometry *(See pages 56–60.)*
  A. Analyze characteristics and properties of two- and three-dimensional shapes and develop mathematical arguments about geometric relationships.
  B. Specify locations and describe spatial relationships using coordinate geometry and other representational systems.
  C. Apply transformations and use symmetry to analyze mathematical situations.
  D. Use visualization, spatial reasoning, and geometric modeling to solve problems.

Standard 4—Measurement *(See pages 61–64.)*
  A. Understand measurable attributes of objects and the units, systems, and processes of measurement.
  B. Apply appropriate techniques, tools, and formulas to determine measurement.

Standard 5—Data Analysis and Probability *(See pages 66–69.)*
  A. Formulate questions that can be addressed with data and collect, organize, and display relevant data to answer them.
  B. Select and use appropriate statistical methods to analyze data.
  C. Develop and evaluate inferences and predictions that are based on data.
  D. Understand and apply basic concepts of probability.

Standard 6—Process *(See pages 70–73.)*
  A. Problem Solving
  B. Reasoning and Proof
  C. Communication
  D. Connections
  E. Representation

Mathematics

1.A

Using Whole Numbers and Expanded Notation
Number and Operations

DIRECTIONS: Choose the best answer.

1. What is the numeral for one million, three hundred fifty two thousand, twenty one?

   Ⓐ 1,535,221

   Ⓑ 15,352,210

   Ⓒ 150,352,021

   Ⓓ 1,352,021

2. What is the word name for 1,382,004?

   Ⓕ one million, three hundred eighty two thousand, four

   Ⓖ one million, three hundred eighty two thousand, four hundred

   Ⓗ one hundred thousand, three hundred eighty two, four

   Ⓙ one hundred million, three hundred eighty two thousand, four hundred

3. Which number is between 456,789 and 562,325?

   Ⓐ 572,325

   Ⓑ 564,331

   Ⓒ 455,644

   Ⓓ 458,319

4. If these numbers are put in order from greatest to least, what is the number exactly in the middle?

   45 55 50 65 30 35 75

   Ⓕ 45

   Ⓖ 50

   Ⓗ 35

   Ⓙ 30

5. How can you write 56,890 in expanded notation?

   Ⓐ 5 + 6 + 8 + 9 + 0 =

   Ⓑ 50,000 + 6,000 + 800 + 90 =

   Ⓒ 56,000 + 8,900 =

   Ⓓ 0.5 + 0.06 + 0.008 + 0.0009 =

6. What is another name for 651?

   Ⓕ 6 thousands, 5 tens, and 1 one

   Ⓖ 6 hundreds, 1 tens, and 5 ones

   Ⓗ 6 tens and 5 ones

   Ⓙ 6 hundreds, 5 tens, and 1 one

7. What is another name for 7 thousands and 5 hundreds?

   Ⓐ 5,700

   Ⓑ 7,050

   Ⓒ 570

   Ⓓ 7,500

8. What is another name for 8 hundreds, 4 tens, and 3 ones?

   Ⓕ 8,430

   Ⓖ 843

   Ⓗ 834

   Ⓙ 8,043

STOP

Mathematics

1.A

Using Fractions and Number Lines

Number and Operations

 Clue Pay close attention to the numbers in the problem and in the answer choices. If you misread even one number, you will probably choose the wrong answer.

DIRECTIONS: Use the number line for questions 1 and 2.

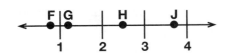

1. What point represents $2\frac{1}{2}$?

   Ⓐ F

   Ⓑ G

   Ⓒ H

   Ⓓ J

2. What point represents $\frac{3}{4}$?

   Ⓕ F

   Ⓖ G

   Ⓗ H

   Ⓙ J

DIRECTIONS: Choose the best answer.

3. What picture shows a fraction equivalent to $\frac{3}{10}$?

4. Which fraction represents 4 divided by 5?

   Ⓕ $\frac{5}{4}$

   Ⓖ $\frac{3}{5}$

   Ⓗ $\frac{4}{5}$

   Ⓙ $\frac{5}{5}$

5. Which fraction tells how much of this figure is shaded?

   Ⓐ $\frac{2}{3}$

   Ⓑ $\frac{3}{4}$

   Ⓒ $\frac{1}{4}$

   Ⓓ $\frac{5}{8}$

6. Which fraction shows how many of the shapes are shaded?

   Ⓕ $\frac{4}{10}$

   Ⓖ $\frac{6}{10}$

   Ⓗ $\frac{7}{10}$

   Ⓙ $\frac{1}{2}$

STOP

Mathematics

1.A

Factors and Multiples
Number and Operations

DIRECTIONS: Choose the best answer.

Clue A **factor** is a number that divides evenly into another number. A **multiple** is the result of a number multiplied by any whole number.

1. **Which of the following expressions does not equal 12?**

   Ⓐ 4×3

   Ⓑ 6×6

   Ⓒ 2×6

   Ⓓ $2 \times 2 \times 3$

2. **Which of the following expressions does not equal 54?**

   Ⓕ 9×6

   Ⓖ 5×4

   Ⓗ 3×18

   Ⓙ 2×27

3. **Which of the following expressions does not equal 20?**

   Ⓐ 20×1

   Ⓑ 4×5

   Ⓒ 2×10

   Ⓓ $2 \times 2 \times 4$

4. **Which of the following expressions does not equal 48?**

   Ⓕ 3×18

   Ⓖ 6×8

   Ⓗ 2×24

   Ⓙ 4×12

5. **Which of the following expressions does not equal 36?**

   Ⓐ 3×11

   Ⓑ 2×18

   Ⓒ 6×6

   Ⓓ $2 \times 2 \times 3 \times 3$

6. **List all factors of 15.**

   Ⓕ 1, 15

   Ⓖ 1, 3, 15

   Ⓗ 1, 3, 5, 15

   Ⓙ 5, 10, 15, 20

7. **List all factors of 24.**

   Ⓐ 1, 2, 6

   Ⓑ 1, 2, 3, 4, 6, 12

   Ⓒ 1, 2, 3, 4, 6, 8, 12, 24

   Ⓓ 0, 1, 2, 3, 4, 5, 6, 12, 14, 24

8. **Complete the table of multiples.**

Multiples of 3	15	18		24			33
Multiples of 4	12	16			28	32	

   What common multiple of 3 and 4 is in the table?

   Ⓕ 21

   Ⓖ 24

   Ⓗ 30

   Ⓙ 33

9. **Complete the table of multiples.**

Multiples of 6	30	36			54	60	
Multiples of 9		27	36			63	

   What common multiples of 6 and 9 are in the table?

   Ⓐ 36 and 54

   Ⓑ 36 and 63

   Ⓒ 27 and 54

   Ⓓ 42 and 54

STOP

Mathematics

| 1.B |

Multiplication and Division
Number and Operations

DIRECTIONS: Choose the best answer.

 Clue You can check your answers in a division problem by multiplying your answer by the divisor.

1. Find 67 × 67.

- (A) 4498
- (B) 5129
- (C) 4489
- (D) 4172

2. Find 185 ÷ 5.

- (F) 37
- (G) 36
- (H) 180
- (J) 190

3. Find 88 ÷ 8.

- (A) 8
- (B) 0
- (C) 1
- (D) 11

4. Find 46 × 82.

- (F) 3,772
- (G) 3,672
- (H) 3,662
- (J) 128

5. Find 444 ÷ 6.

- (A) 78
- (B) 63
- (C) 74
- (D) 64

6. Find 22 × 12.

- (F) 240
- (G) 264
- (H) 242
- (J) 44

7. Find 34 × 57.

- (A) 91
- (B) 1,918
- (C) 1,938
- (D) 2,451

8. Find 42 ÷ 7.

- (F) 49
- (G) 294
- (H) 35
- (J) 6

9. Find 45 × 32.

- (A) 1,440
- (B) 1,120
- (C) 77
- (D) 1,395

10. Find 464 ÷ 4.

- (F) 460
- (G) 468
- (H) 116
- (J) 232

STOP

Name _____ Date _____

Mathematics

| 1.C |

Addition and Subtraction
Number and Operations

DIRECTIONS: Add the numbers.

1.
$$362$$
$$+\ 119$$

2.
$$428$$
$$+\ 358$$

3.
$$524$$
$$+\ 167$$

4.
$$665$$
$$+\ 219$$

5.
$$92$$
$$29$$
$$+\ 64$$

6.
$$85$$
$$27$$
$$+\ 78$$

7.
$$38$$
$$25$$
$$+\ 63$$

8.
$$51$$
$$49$$
$$+\ 73$$

DIRECTIONS: Subtract the numbers.

9.
$$96$$
$$-\ 27$$

10.
$$35$$
$$-\ 19$$

11.
$$87$$
$$-\ 68$$

12.
$$45$$
$$-\ 18$$

13.
$$311$$
$$-\ 127$$

14.
$$422$$
$$-\ 158$$

15.
$$535$$
$$-\ 348$$

16.
$$723$$
$$-\ 158$$

STOP

Mathematics

2.A

Identifying and Extending Patterns
Algebra

DIRECTIONS: Find the pattern in each row of numbers. Continue the pattern to fill in the blanks. Then, match the pattern to the correct rule.

Pattern	**Rule**
1. 1, 3, 5, ___, ___, 11, 13	−11
2. 70, ___, 50, ___, ___, 20, 10	+12
3. 1, 8, 15, 22, ___, ___, ___	+8
4. 36, 33, 30, ___, ___, ___, ___	−9
5. 115, 100, 85, ___, ___, ___, ___	+2
6. 64, 55, 46, ___, ___, ___, ___	−10
7. 17, 25, 33, ___, ___, ___, ___	−3
8. 96, ___, 84, 78, ___, ___, ___	−15
9. 88, ___, 66, ___, 44, ___, ___	−6
10. 12, 24, 36, ___, ___, ___, ___	+7

11. If you were to continue Pattern 3, what would be the next three numbers in the pattern?

_____

12. If you were to continue Pattern 8, what would be the next three numbers in the pattern?

_____

STOP

Mathematics

2.B

Working With Variables
Algebra

DIRECTIONS: Choose a variable for the unknown amount. Then, write a number sentence to represent the problem. Finally, find the solution.

> **Example:**
>
> Kyle made a dozen cookies. His little sister ate 5 of them. How many cookies are left?
>
> Variable: Let c = number of cookies left
> Number sentence: $c + 5 = 12$
> Solution: $c = 7$

 Clue

A **variable** is an amount that is not known. It is often represented by a letter. Variables are used in number sentences to represent a situation.

1. **Julie is playing a board game. She rolls a 3 on the first die. What must she roll on the second die to move 9 spaces?**

    Variable: _____

    Number sentence: _____

    Solution: _____

2. **Jacob has a bag with 4 pieces of candy. His father puts another handful into the bag. Jacob then has 13 pieces. How many pieces did his father give him?**

    Variable: _____

    Number sentence: _____

    Solution: _____

3. **A factory has 314 workers. The owner gave each worker a bonus of $500. What was the total amount of bonus that the owner gave his workers?**

    Variable: _____

    Number sentence: _____

    Solution: _____

4. **Kayla's cat had 7 kittens. So far, she has given away 5 of them. How many kittens are left?**

    Variable: _____

    Number sentence: _____

    Solution: _____

STOP

Mathematics

2.B

Commutative and Associative Properties
Algebra

Examples:

The **commutative property** says you can switch the order of the numbers and still get the same answer.

$$5 + 10 = 10 + 5$$ $$5 \times 2 = 2 \times 5$$
$$15 = 15$$ $$10 = 10$$

The **associative property** says you can change the grouping of the numbers and still get the same answer.

$$(3 + 5) + 6 = 3 + (5 + 6)$$ $$(3 \times 5) \times 6 = 3 \times (5 \times 6)$$
$$8 + 6 = 3 + 11$$ $$15 \times 6 = 3 \times 30$$
$$14 = 14$$ $$90 = 90$$

DIRECTIONS: Identify the property that makes each of these number sentences true. Write **A** for the associative property or **C** for the commutative property.

_____ 1. $59 + 43 = 43 + 59$

_____ 2. $(7 + 8) + 6 = 7 + (8 + 6)$

_____ 3. $(5 + 2) + 3 = 3 + (5 + 2)$

_____ 4. $5 \times (8 \times 6) = (5 \times 8) \times 6$

_____ 5. $3 \times 2 = 2 \times 3$

_____ 6. $412 \times (13 \times 15) = 412 \times (15 \times 13)$

DIRECTIONS: Rewrite each of the expressions in an equivalent form using the property indicated.

7. $4 \times 3 =$ _____ commutative

8. $5 + 8 + 6 =$ _____ commutative

9. $7 \times (4 \times 3) =$ _____ associative

10. $7 \times (4 \times 3) =$ _____ commutative

11. $(8 + 4) + 2 =$ _____ associative

12. $(8 + 4) + 2 =$ _____ commutative

STOP

Mathematics

| 2.C |

Using Data to Draw Conclusions
Algebra

DIRECTIONS: One way to organize data is to use a **tally chart.** One mark is used for each number, and a slash is drawn through every 4 marks to represent 5. The crossing guards at Howell Elementary are concerned that a large number of cars cross a street that they do not monitor. They are using a tally chart to help present their findings to the principal. Answer the following questions based on the tally chart below.

1. **What is the least number of cars that crossed Johnson Avenue in one day?**

_____

2. **What is the greatest number of cars that crossed Johnson Avenue in one day?**

_____

3. **Which day had the least number of cars?**

_____

4. **What is the total number of cars that crossed from Monday through Friday?**

_____

5. **The principal may allow an extra crossing guard for one day of the week. Which day should the crossing guards recommend?**

_____

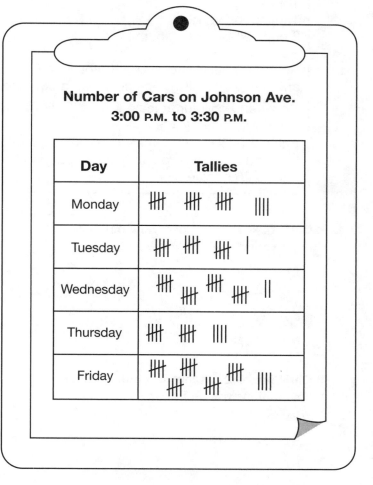

Number of Cars on Johnson Ave.
3:00 P.M. to 3:30 P.M.

Day	Tallies
Monday	﷽ ﷽ ﷽ ||||
Tuesday	﷽ ﷽ ﷽ |
Wednesday	﷽ ﷽ ﷽ ||
Thursday	﷽ ﷽ ||||
Friday	﷽ ﷽ ﷽ ﷽ ﷽ ﷽ ||||

STOP

Mathematics

2.D

Quantity and Change
Algebra

DIRECTIONS: This is Chris's favorite sugar cookie recipe. Use it to answer the questions.

Sugar Cookies

$\frac{1}{3}$ cup butter or margarine, softened

$\frac{1}{3}$ cup shortening

$\frac{3}{4}$ cup sugar

1 teaspoon baking powder
pinch salt
1 egg
1 teaspoon vanilla
2 cups all-purpose flour

Beat butter and shortening thoroughly. Add sugar, baking powder and a pinch of salt and mix until well combined. Beat in egg and vanilla and flour.

Cover and chill for at least 1 hour. Split the dough in $\frac{1}{2}$ and roll one half at a time. Cut out with cookie cutters.

Bake at 325°F on ungreased cookie sheets for about 7 to 8 minutes, until edges are firm and bottoms are lightly browned (don't overcook).

Makes 36 cookies.

---

1. **If Chris bakes 36 cookies, how much flour does he need?**

   Ⓐ 1 cup

   Ⓑ $1\frac{1}{2}$ cups

   Ⓒ 2 cups

   Ⓓ 3 cups

2. **If Chris bakes 2 batches of cookies, how many cookies will he bake?**

   Ⓕ 66

   Ⓖ 72

   Ⓗ 76

   Ⓙ 84

3. **How much flour will he need to bake the 2 batches of cookies?**

   Ⓐ 2 cups

   Ⓑ $2\frac{1}{2}$ cups

   Ⓒ 3 cups

   Ⓓ 4 cups

4. **Chris needs to bake 3 batches of cookies for a party. How much butter or margarine will he use?**

   Ⓕ $\frac{1}{3}$ cup

   Ⓖ $\frac{2}{3}$ cup

   Ⓗ 1 cup

   Ⓙ 3 cups

STOP

Mathematics

1.0–2.0

For pages 45–54

Mini-Test 1

Number and Operations; Algebra

DIRECTIONS: Choose the best answer.

1. **What is the numeral for four million, eight hundred two thousand, sixteen?**

   Ⓐ 4,802,160

   Ⓑ 4,082,016

   Ⓒ 4,802,016

   Ⓓ 4,802,160

2. **Joaquim is eating a pizza. The pizza has eight slices and Joaquim eats five. What fraction of the pizza did Joaquim eat?**

   Ⓕ $\frac{1}{8}$ Ⓗ $\frac{2}{8}$

   Ⓖ $\frac{3}{8}$ Ⓙ $\frac{5}{8}$

3. **On a number line, is $\frac{2}{3}$ to the right or left of $1\frac{1}{2}$?**

   _____

4. **Find 278 + 146.**

   Ⓐ 132

   Ⓑ 324

   Ⓒ 414

   Ⓓ 424

5. **Find 794 − 318.**

   Ⓕ 394

   Ⓖ 484

   Ⓗ 476

   Ⓙ 1,112

6. **Find 78 × 84.**

   Ⓐ 262

   Ⓑ 94

   Ⓒ 6,552

   Ⓓ 1,424

7. **Find 243 ÷ 9.**

   Ⓕ 27

   Ⓖ 17

   Ⓗ 26

   Ⓙ 2,187

8. **4 × 6 = 6 × 4 is an example of which property?**

   Ⓐ associative

   Ⓑ commutative

   Ⓒ distributive

   Ⓓ inverse

9. **Extend the number pattern.**
   1, 4, 7, 10, 13, 16, 19, ___

   Ⓕ 1

   Ⓖ 22

   Ⓗ 20

   Ⓙ 16

10. **In the number sentence $x + 8 = 17$, what is x?**

    Ⓐ 8

    Ⓑ 9

    Ⓒ 10

    Ⓓ 11

11. **List all factors of 10.**

    Ⓕ 1, 10

    Ⓖ 1, 2, 10

    Ⓗ 1, 2, 5, 10

    Ⓙ 0, 1, 2, 5, 10

STOP

Mathematics

| 3.A |

Identifying Quadrilaterals
Geometry

DIRECTIONS: Classify the shapes below as **quadrilateral, trapezoid, parallelogram, rectangle, square,** or **rhombus.**

A **quadrilateral** is any figure with 4 sides and 4 angles. Some quadrilaterals have special names.

Trapezoid—a quadrilateral with 1 set of parallel sides

Parallelogram—a quadrilateral with 2 sets of parallel sides and opposite sides of equal length

Rectangle—a quadrilateral with 4 right angles and opposite sides of equal length

Square—a quadrilateral with 4 right angles and 4 equal sides

Rhombus—a quadrilateral with 4 equal sides and 2 pairs of parallel sides

1.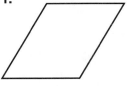

_____

2.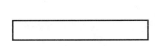

_____

3.

_____

4.

_____

5.

_____

6.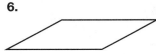

_____

7.

_____

8.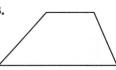

_____

9.

_____

10.

_____

11.

_____

12.

_____

STOP

Name _____ Date _____

Mathematics

Identifying Triangles
Geometry

DIRECTIONS: Choose the best answer.

Example:

Triangles can be sorted by either their sides or their angles.		
Equilateral triangle—All 3 sides are the same length.	**Isosceles triangle**—Only 2 sides are the same length. 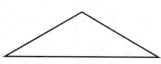	**Scalene triangle**—None of the sides are the same length. 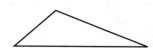
Right Triangle—One of the angles measures 90 degrees (an L-shaped angle).	**Acute Triangle**—All three angles in the triangle measure less than 90 degrees. 	**Obtuse Triangle**—One of the angles measures more than 90 degrees. 

1. This is a(n) _____ triangle.

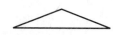

   (A)   equilateral

   (B)   isosceles

   (C)   scalene

   (D)   none of the above

2. This is a(n) _____ triangle.

   (F)   equilateral

   (G)   isosceles

   (H)   scalene

   (J)   none of the above

3. This is a(n) _____ triangle.

   (A)   equilateral

   (B)   isosceles

   (C)   scalene

   (D)   none of the above

4. This is a(n) _____ triangle.

   (F)   right

   (G)   acute

   (H)   obtuse

   (J)   none of the above

5. This is a(n) _____ triangle.

   (A)   right

   (B)   acute

   (C)   obtuse

   (D)   none of the above

6. This is a(n) _____ triangle.

   (F)   right

   (G)   acute

   (H)   obtuse

   (J)   none of the above

Mathematics

3.B

Using Coordinates
Geometry

DIRECTIONS: The students in Room 14 are going on a scavenger hunt at Willow Lake. Each team needs to find the objects below. Write the item from the word list that is found at each coordinate.

Clue   Remember that the first number of an ordered pair is the number on the *x*-axis.

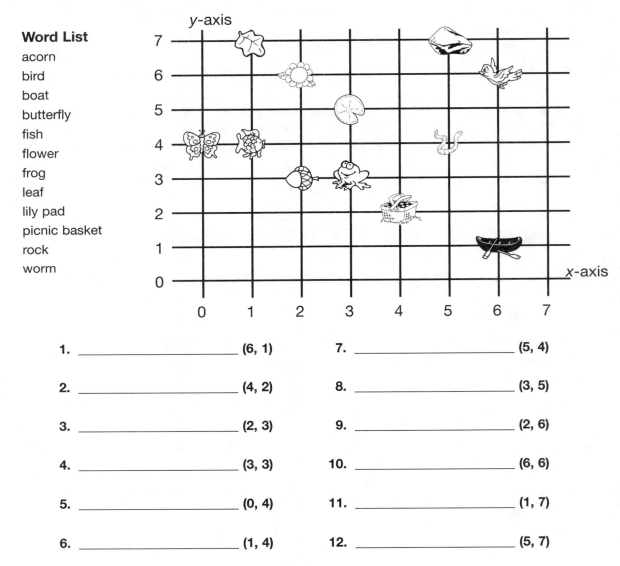

Word List
acorn
bird
boat
butterfly
fish
flower
frog
leaf
lily pad
picnic basket
rock
worm

1. _____ (6, 1)

2. _____ (4, 2)

3. _____ (2, 3)

4. _____ (3, 3)

5. _____ (0, 4)

6. _____ (1, 4)

7. _____ (5, 4)

8. _____ (3, 5)

9. _____ (2, 6)

10. _____ (6, 6)

11. _____ (1, 7)

12. _____ (5, 7)

DIRECTIONS: After the scavenger hunt, the students will have a picnic. Help them get ready for the picnic by drawing the given shapes at each coordinate.

13. **banana (0, 0)**

14. **sandwich (7, 4)**

15. **kite (3, 4)**

16. **carrot (1, 2)**

Mathematics

3.C

Lines of Symmetry
Geometry

DIRECTIONS: Choose the best answer.

Examples:

An object or shape has a **line of symmetry** when the two sides can be folded along a line and match up perfectly. Each side is a mirror image of the other. For example:

This diamond has two lines of symmetry.

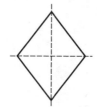

This arrow has one line of symmetry.

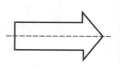

---

1. **Which of the figures below does not show a line of symmetry?**

   Ⓐ

   Ⓒ

   Ⓑ

   Ⓓ

2. **Which of these letters has a line of symmetry?**

   Ⓕ **Q**

   Ⓖ **P**

   Ⓗ **N**

   Ⓙ **M**

3. **Look at the letters below. Which one does not have a line of symmetry?**

   Ⓐ **O**

   Ⓑ **T**

   Ⓒ **G**

   Ⓓ **X**

4. **Which of the figures below does not have a line of symmetry?**

   Ⓕ

   Ⓖ

   Ⓗ

   Ⓙ

STOP

Mathematics

3.D

Using Geometric Shapes
Geometry

DIRECTIONS: In the space below, use any combination of these basic geometric shapes to create a drawing of a real-life person, place, or thing.

 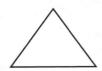

Mathematics

| 4.A |

Selecting Units of Measure
Measurement

DIRECTIONS: Show which units would be best to measure these items by writing the letter of the appropriate units next to each item. Each unit should be used only once.

_____ 1. one apple   a. yards

_____ 2. short distance races   b. ounces

_____ 3. distance between cities   c. feet

_____ 4. a jug of milk   d. miles

_____ 5. size of a room   e. gallons

_____ 6. liquid baby medicine   a. kiloliters

_____ 7. height of a book   b. milligrams

_____ 8. amount of water in a water tower   c. milliliters

_____ 9. towing capacity of a truck   d. kilograms

_____ 10. amount of medicine in a pill   e. centimeters

_____ 11. amount of time you sleep each night a. degrees

_____ 12. length of time you brush your teeth b. tons

_____ 13. how cold it is outside   c. minutes

_____ 14. how much a truck weighs   d. hours

STOP

Name _____ Date _____

Mathematics

| 4.A |

Converting U.S. Customary Measurements

Measurement

DIRECTIONS: Fill in the blanks with the equivalent measurement. Use the conversion chart below to help you find your answers.

Length:
1 foot = 12 inches
1 yard = 3 feet
1 mile = 5,280 feet

1. **7 yards =** _____ **feet**

2. **24 inches =** _____ **feet**

3. **6 feet =** _____ **yard(s)**

4. **10 miles =** _____ **feet**

5. **60 inches =** _____ **feet**

DIRECTIONS: Fill in the blanks with the equivalent measurement. Use the conversion chart below to help you find your answers.

Capacity:
1 tablespoon = 3 teaspoons
1 cup = 16 tablespoons = 8 fluid ounces
1 pint = 2 cups
1 quart = 2 pints
1 gallon = 4 quarts

6. **8 gallons =** _____ **quarts**

7. **28 quarts =** _____ **pints**

8. **10 pints =** _____ **cups**

9. **18 cups =** _____ **pints**

10. **4 tablespoons =** _____ **teaspoons**

11. **24 quarts =** _____ **gallons**

12. **2 cups =** _____ **fluid ounces**

13. **9 teaspoons =** _____ **tablespoons**

14. **2 cups =** _____ **tablespoons**

DIRECTIONS: Fill in the blanks with the equivalent measurement. Use the conversion chart below to help you find your answers.

Weight:
1 pound (lb.) = 16 ounces (oz.)
1 ton (t.) = 2,000 pounds (lbs.)

15. **2 lbs. =** _____ **oz.**

16. **160 oz. =** _____ **lbs.**

17. **15 lbs. =** _____ **oz.**

18. **4,000 lbs. =** _____ **t.**

19. **6 t. =** _____ **lbs.**

20. **64 oz. =** _____ **lbs.**

STOP

Mathematics

4.B

Finding the Perimeter
Measurement

DIRECTIONS: Choose the best answer.

Example:

Perimeter is the distance around the edge of a shape. You can find the perimeter by using this formula: (2 × length) + (2 × width). For example, this rectangle has a length of 18 and width of 5. To find the perimeter:

$2 \times 18 = 36$
$2 \times 5 = 10$
$36 + 10 = 46$

Width = 5

Length = 18

1. A rectangle has a length of 2 and width of 27. What is the perimeter?
   - (A) 29
   - (B) 58
   - (C) 25
   - (D) 54

2. A rectangle has a length of 3 and width of 18. What is the perimeter?
   - (F) 21
   - (G) 54
   - (H) 42
   - (J) 15

3. A rectangle has a length of 12 and width of 36. What is the perimeter?
   - (A) 48
   - (B) 96
   - (C) 74
   - (D) 76

4. A rectangle has a length of 15 and width of 24. What is the perimeter?
   - (F) 54
   - (G) 39
   - (H) 62
   - (J) 78

5. A rectangle has a length of 4 and width of 18. What is the perimeter?
   - (A) 22
   - (B) 14
   - (C) 44
   - (D) 36

6. A rectangle has a length of 20 and width of 30. What is the perimeter?
   - (F) 50
   - (G) 100
   - (H) 80
   - (J) 70

7. A rectangle has a length of 6 and width of 12. What is the perimeter?
   - (A) 36
   - (B) 18
   - (C) 6
   - (D) 78

8. A rectangle has a length of 8 and width of 9. What is the perimeter?
   - (F) 17
   - (G) 1
   - (H) 80
   - (J) 34

STOP

Mathematics

4.B

Finding the Volume
Measurement

DIRECTIONS: Use the formula to determine the volume of the figures below. Match each figure to its correct volume.

Clue

One way to find volume is to use the following rule:
Volume = length × width × height.

1.

height = _____   width = _____

length = _____

20 cubic units

2.

width = _____

height = _____

length = _____

16 cubic units

3.

height = _____   width = _____

length = _____

12 cubic units

4.

height = _____   width = _____

length = _____

18 cubic units

5.

height = _____   width = _____

length = _____

24 cubic units

STOP

Name _____   Date _____

Mini-Test 2

Geometry; Measurement

1. **This is a(n) _____ triangle.**

   Ⓐ equilateral
   Ⓑ isosceles
   Ⓒ scalene
   Ⓓ none of the above

2. **This quadrilateral is called a _____ .**

   Ⓕ parallelogram
   Ⓖ trapezoid
   Ⓗ rhombus
   Ⓙ rectangle

3. **A quadrilateral with one set of parallel sides is a _____ .**

   Ⓐ parallelogram
   Ⓑ trapezoid
   Ⓒ rhombus
   Ⓓ rectangle

4. **Which of these letters has a line of symmetry?**

   Ⓕ **C**
   Ⓖ **R**
   Ⓗ **S**
   Ⓙ **F**

5. **A rectangle with a length of 3 and width of 4 has an area of 12. What is the perimeter?**

   Ⓐ 7
   Ⓑ 14
   Ⓒ 48
   Ⓓ 12

6. **A rectangular prism has a length of 6 cubic units, a width of 2 cubic units, and a height of 3 cubic units. What is the volume?**

   Ⓕ 11 cubic units
   Ⓖ 15 cubic units
   Ⓗ 22 cubic units
   Ⓙ 36 cubic units

7. **If you wanted to measure the length of a football field, what unit would you most likely use?**

   Ⓐ inches
   Ⓑ centimeters
   Ⓒ yards
   Ⓓ miles

8. **Barb used 8 quarts of water when she washed her hands and face. How many pints of water did she use?**

   Ⓕ 8 pints
   Ⓖ 16 pints
   Ⓗ 24 pints
   Ⓙ 32 pints

9. **A truck has 6 tons of cargo. How many pounds is that?**

   Ⓐ 12,000 pounds
   Ⓑ 1,200 pounds
   Ⓒ 120 pounds
   Ⓓ 12 pounds

STOP

Name _____ Date _____

Representing Data
Data Analysis and Probability

DIRECTIONS: The data below shows a person's heart rate while jogging. Use the data to make both a line graph and a bar graph and to answer the questions.

Clue

An **interval** is the amount of time between two events. On these graphs, it is the time between each heart rate. For example, the first interval on these graphs is from 0 to 5 minutes.

Data

Time	Heart Rate
0 min.	80
5 min.	120
10 min.	135
15 min.	148
20 min.	159
25 min.	150

1. **Line Graph**
Heart Rate While Jogging

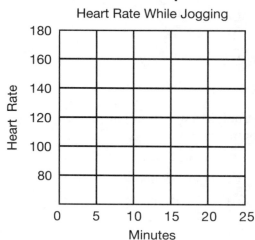

2. **Bar Graph**
Heart Rate While Jogging

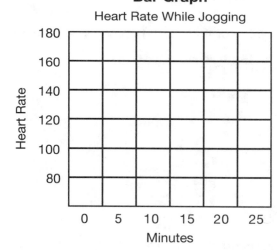

3. At what time was the jogger's heart rate the highest?_____

4. During which time interval did the jogger's heart rate increase the most?_____

5. During which time interval did the jogger's heart rate increase the least?_____

6. During which interval did the jogger's heart rate decrease?_____

STOP

Mathematics

5.B

Describing and Comparing Data
Data Analysis and Probability

DIRECTIONS: The tally chart shows the hair color of some fourth-grade students. Choose the best answer.

Brown	Black	Blond	Red

1. Which of these questions could you answer using the information on the tally chart?

(A)   How often do the students get their hair cut?

(B)   How many students dye their hair?

(C)   Which students have long hair?

(D)   How many more brown-haired students are there than blond-haired students?

2. Which graph below best represents the data on the tally chart?

(F)

Brown Black Blond Red

(H)
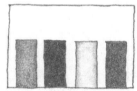
Brown Black Blond Red

(G)
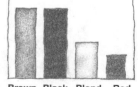
Brown Black Blond Red

(J)
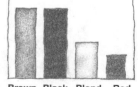
Brown Black Blond Red

3. Which circle shows the fraction of the students on the tally chart that have black hair?

(A)
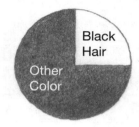
Black Hair / Other Color

(B)
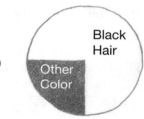
Black Hair / Other Color

(C)

Other Color / Black Hair

(D)
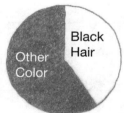
Black Hair / Other Color

STOP

Name _____ Date _____

Mathematics

Developing and Testing Predictions

Data Analysis and Probability

DIRECTIONS: Roll a die 60 times. Record the results of your experiment below.

1. **Predict how often you expect to roll each number.**

   _____

   _____

   _____

   _____

2. **Predict how often you expect to roll an even number.**

   _____

   _____

   _____

   _____

3. **Predict how often you expect to roll an odd number.**

   _____

   _____

   _____

4. **Number of times you rolled a 1:**

   _____

5. **Number of times you rolled a 2:**

   _____

6. **Number of times you rolled a 3:**

   _____

7. **Number of times you rolled a 4:**

   _____

8. **Number of times you rolled a 5:**

   _____

9. **Number of times you rolled a 6:**

   _____

10. **How do your actual results compare with the results you predicted?**

    _____

    _____

    _____

    _____

    _____

    _____

    _____

Mathematics

5.D

Determining Likelihood of Outcomes
Data Analysis and Probability

DIRECTIONS: Look at the spinner. Identify as **certain**, **likely**, **unlikely**, or **impossible** the probability that the arrow will land on:

1. a number. _____

2. an 8. _____

3. a circle. _____

4. a shape. _____

5. a triangle. _____

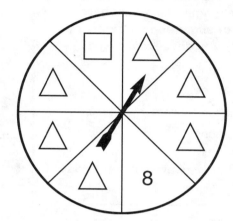

DIRECTIONS: Look at the spinner. Identify as **certain**, **likely**, **unlikely**, or **impossible** the probability that the arrow will land on:

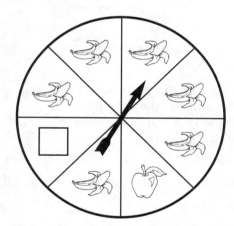

6. a banana. _____

7. a fruit. _____

8. a star. _____

9. a triangle. _____

10. an apple. _____

DIRECTIONS: Look at the spinner. Identify as **certain**, **likely**, **unlikely**, or **impossible** the probability that the arrow will land on:

11. a 5. _____

12. an odd number. _____

13. a triangle. _____

14. a 2. _____

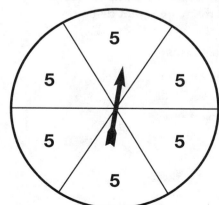

STOP

Mathematics

| 6.A |

Solving Problems
Process

DIRECTIONS: Read and work each problem. Choose the best answer.

1. Grant went to get a frozen yogurt from the concession stand. He could choose vanilla, chocolate, or twist yogurt. He could have a cup, wafer cone, or sugar cone. How many possible combinations does Grant have?

(A) 6 combinations

(B) 3 combinations

(C) 8 combinations

(D) 9 combinations

2. How many more tickets were sold on Friday than on Tuesday?

CENTER CINEMAS
MOVIE TICKET SALES

MONDAY
TUESDAY
WEDNESDAY
THURSDAY
FRIDAY

KEY: 10 TICKETS =

(F) 45 tickets

(G) 55 tickets

(H) 75 tickets

(J) 295 tickets

3. A store has 3,802 compact discs on the shelves. The store receives 2 new cases of compact discs. There are 320 compact discs in each case. How many compact discs does the store have now?

(A) 640 compact discs

(B) 3,802 compact discs

(C) 4,442 compact discs

(D) 3,482 compact discs

4. If you wanted to compare the features of two different solid shapes, the best thing to use would be a _____ .

(F) Venn diagram

(G) pie chart

(H) tally chart

(J) line graph

5. Larry, Carey, and Harry went out for lunch. Each friend ordered a salad. The choices were egg, tuna, and chicken. Carey won't eat egg. Larry never orders tuna. Harry only likes chicken. Each friend ate something different. Who ordered tuna?

(A) Larry

(B) Carey

(C) Harry

(D) not enough information

6. A worker at Command Software makes $720 a week. You want to figure out how much he makes an hour. What other piece of information do you need?

(F) the number of weeks he works each year

(G) the number of vacation days he takes

(H) how much money he makes each day

(J) how many hours a week he works

7. You have coins that total $1.23. What coins do you have?

(A) 10 dimes, 1 nickel, 3 pennies

(B) 3 quarters, 3 dimes, 3 pennies

(C) 4 quarters, 1 dime, 2 nickels, 3 pennies

(D) 4 quarters, 3 dimes, 3 pennies

STOP

Name _____   Date _____

6.B

Evaluating Mathematical Arguments
Process

DIRECTIONS: Choose the best answer.

Clue   Before you choose an answer, ask yourself, "Does this answer make sense?"

1. **Which of the following would you probably measure in feet?**

   (A) length of a pencil

   (B) distance between two cities

   (C) amount of juice left in a bottle

   (D) the length of a couch

2. **You are mailing your brother's college application today. It is a regular letter size. You must make sure you have enough postage. How much do you think it weighs?**

   (F) 1 pound   (H) 1 ounce

   (G) 8 pounds   (J) 8 ounces

3. **A yard is surrounded by 400 feet of fence. It took Lynne 8 days to paint the fence. Which number sentence can Lynne use to figure out how much fence she painted in a day?**

   (A) $400 \times 8 = \blacksquare$

   (B) $400 \div 8 = \blacksquare$

   (C) $400 - 8 = \blacksquare$

   (D) $400 + 8 = \blacksquare$

4. **Five students want to find their average height in inches. Their heights are 54 inches, 56 inches, 52 inches, 57 inches, and 53 inches. How would you find the average height of the students?**

   (F) Add the heights and multiply by 5.

   (G) Add the heights and divide by 5.

   (H) Add the heights and divide by the number of inches in 1 foot.

   (J) Multiply the heights and divide by the number of inches in 1 foot.

5. **Mr. Cook was 25 years old when Mary was born. How old will he be when Mary has her thirteenth birthday?**

   (A) 38 years old

   (B) 12 years old

   (C) 25 years old

   (D) 13 years old

6. **Write a number sentence to verify your answer to question 5.**

   _____

   _____

   _____

7. **Marcos has $47.82. He plans to spend $25 on presents. How much money will he have left, to the nearest dollar?**

   (F) $22

   (G) $22.82

   (H) $23

   (J) $25

8. **Write a number sentence to verify the answer to question 7.**

   _____

   _____

   _____

STOP

Mathematics

6.C

Using Mathematical Language
Process

DIRECTIONS: Describe how to solve each problem in the space provided.

1. If you burn 318 calories in 60 minutes of playing tennis, how many calories would you burn in 30 minutes? _____

2. A chicken pot pie was cut into 8 slices. For dinner, the Wilsons ate $\frac{3}{8}$ of the pie. For lunch, the Wilsons ate $\frac{1}{4}$ of the pie. How much of the pie was eaten? _____

3. There were 488 balloons decorating the gymnasium for a party. There were 97 students at the party. If each student brought home an equal number of balloons after the party, how many balloons were left over? _____

4. A roller coaster holds a total of 184 people. If each car holds 8 people, how many cars are there? _____

5. Jesse bought a pack of cards for $1.25 and a baseball for $8.39. He has $5.36 left over. How much money did he start with?
_____

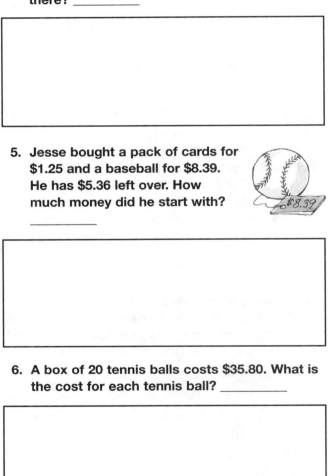

6. A box of 20 tennis balls costs $35.80. What is the cost for each tennis ball? _____

STOP

Name _____ Date _____

6.D/6.E

Connecting and Representing Mathematical Ideas
Process

DIRECTIONS: Choose the best answer.

1. The school basketball team has scored a total of 369 points during 9 games so far this season. What was the average number of points scored per game?

   (A) 47 points

   (B) 360 points

   (C) 40 points

   (D) 41 points

2. Garth took $15.00 to the art supply store. He spent $12.76 on art supplies. He wants to buy one more item that costs $2.50. Does he have enough money?

   (F) yes

   (G) no

3. A dripping faucet leaks 3 gallons of water each day. If the faucet leaks for 20 days before it is fixed, and the price of water is $0.30 per gallon, how much did the leak cost?

   (A) $10.50

   (B) $1.80

   (C) $18.00

   (D) $24.50

4. Rita left dance class at 3:30 P.M. She arrived home at 4:17 P.M. How long did it take Rita to get home?

   (F) 1 hour, 17 minutes

   (G) 47 minutes

   (H) 37 minutes

   (J) 13 minutes

5. Rayna wants to buy a toy that costs $1.39. She has the coins below. How much more does she need?

   (A) $1.04

   (B) 69¢

   (C) 70¢

   (D) $1.05

6. Which of the following sets of figures shows $\frac{1}{3}$ shaded?

   (F) ①①①①●●●●

   (G) ①①●●●●①

   (H) ①●①●①●

   (J) ①①●①①●

7. In the picture below, 1 book stands for 5 books. How many books does this picture stand for?

   (A) 25

   (B) 45

   (C) 40

   (D) 30

STOP

Mathematics

| 5.0–6.0 |

For pages 66–73

Mini-Test 3

Data Analysis and Probability; Process

DIRECTIONS: Use the graph below for questions 1–2.

Favorite Vacation Destination

Beach	🕶🕶🕶
Water Park	🕶🕶🕶🕶
Amusement Park	🕶🕶🕶🕶🕶

Key: 🕶 = 8 votes

1. For how many votes does one symbol stand?

- (A) 2 votes
- (B) 5 votes
- (C) 6 votes
- (D) 8 votes

2. How many more people would rather go to an amusement park than the beach?

- (F) 10 people
- (G) 12 people
- (H) 20 people
- (J) 22 people

DIRECTIONS: Choose the best answer.

3. Aidan bought a slice of pizza and a soda at the arcade. The pizza cost $4.50, and the soda cost $2.75. Aidan paid with a ten dollar bill. How much change did he receive?

- (A) $5.50
- (B) $3.00
- (C) $2.75
- (D) $7.25

4. A bag contains 7 red marbles, 3 white marbles, and 2 green marbles. The probability of picking a blue marble is _____ .

- (F) certain
- (G) impossible
- (H) likely
- (J) unlikely

DIRECTIONS: Use the information below to help you solve questions 5–7.

🍬 🍬 🍬 🍬
🍬 🍬 🍬

You have a bag of candy to share with your class. There are 25 students in your class. You want each student to get 7 pieces.

5. What operation will you need to use to figure out how many candies you need?

- (A) addition
- (B) subtraction
- (C) multiplication
- (D) division

6. How many candies do you need in all?

- (F) 200 candies
- (G) 175 candies
- (H) 1,500 candies
- (J) 145 candies

7. Two students are absent on the day you hand out the candies. Write a number sentence to show how many candies you will have left over.

_____

_____

STOP

How Am I Doing?

Mini-Test 1

Page 55

Number Correct

10–11 answers correct	**Great Job!** Move on to the section test on page 76.
6–9 answers correct	**You're almost there!** But you still need a little practice. Review practice pages 45–54 before moving on to the section test on page 76.
0–5 answers correct	**Oops!** Time to review what you have learned and try again. Review the practice section on pages 45–54. Then, retake the test on page 55. Now, move on to the section test on page 76.

Mini-Test 2

Page 65

Number Correct

9 answers correct	**Awesome!** Move on to the section test on page 76.
6–8 answers correct	**You're almost there!** But you still need a little practice. Review practice pages 56–64 before moving on to the section test on page 76.
0–5 answers correct	**Oops!** Time to review what you have learned and try again. Review the practice section on pages 56–64. Then, retake the test on page 65. Now, move on to the section test on page 76.

Mini-Test 3

Page 74

Number Correct

7 answers correct	**Great Job!** Move on to the section test on page 76.
4–6 answers correct	**You're almost there!** But you still need a little practice. Review practice pages 66–73 before moving on to the section test on page 76.
0–3 answers correct	**Oops!** Time to review what you have learned and try again. Review the practice section on pages 66–73. Then, retake the test on page 74. Now, move on to the section test on page 76.

Final Mathematics Test
For pages 45–74

DIRECTIONS: Choose the best answer.

1. **What is the word name for 6,703,405?**
   - (A) six million, seven zero three thousand, four hundred five
   - (B) six million, seven hundred three thousand, four hundred fifty
   - (C) six million, seven hundred three thousand, four hundred five
   - (D) six million, seven hundred three, four hundred five

2. **How can you write 9,876 in expanded notation?**
   - (F) 9,800 + 76 + 0
   - (G) 9,800 + 70 + 60
   - (H) 9,000 + 870 + 60
   - (J) 9,000 + 800 + 70 + 6

3. **What fraction of the shape is shaded?**

   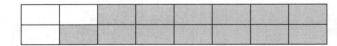

   - (A) $\frac{13}{16}$
   - (B) $\frac{3}{16}$
   - (C) $\frac{3}{8}$
   - (D) $\frac{5}{16}$

4. **Which of the following expressions does not equal 24?**
   - (F) 8×3
   - (G) 4×6
   - (H) 2×12
   - (J) $2 \times 2 \times 3$

5. **List all factors of 12.**
   - (A) 1, 12
   - (B) 1, 2, 6, 12
   - (C) 1, 3, 4, 6, 12
   - (D) 1, 2, 3, 4, 6, 12

6. **Find 75 + 36 + 24.**
   - (F) 81
   - (G) 15
   - (H) 111
   - (J) 135

7. **Find 96 − 48.**
   - (A) 144
   - (B) 92
   - (C) 48
   - (D) 47

8. **Find 54 × 73.**
   - (F) 3,942
   - (G) 2,478
   - (H) 1,062
   - (J) 427

9. **Find 847 ÷ 7.**
   - (A) 847
   - (B) 121
   - (C) 127
   - (D) 221

GO

Name _____   Date _____

DIRECTIONS: Choose the best answer.

10. Find the missing number.

18, 26, 34, _____ , 50, 58

- (F) 38
- (G) 40
- (H) 42
- (J) 44

11. Extend the number pattern.

56, 53, 50, 47, 44, _____

- (A) 40
- (B) 41
- (C) 43
- (D) 45

12. Which property says that you can switch the order of the numbers and still get the same answer?

- (F) inverse
- (G) associative
- (H) commutative
- (J) distributive

13. A quadrilateral with 4 right angles and 4 equal sides is a _____ .

- (A) rectangle
- (B) square
- (C) rhombus
- (D) trapezoid

14. This is a(n) _____ triangle.

- (F) equilateral
- (G) isosceles
- (H) scalene
- (J) none of the above

DIRECTIONS: Use the graph below to answer questions 15 and 16.

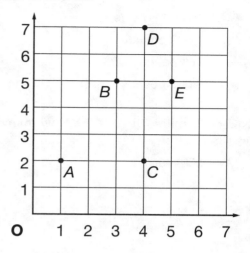

15. What are the coordinates of point *A*?

- (A) (2, 1)
- (B) (1, 2)
- (C) (1, 1)
- (D) (2, 2)

16. What are the coordinates of point *B*?

- (F) (4, 2)
- (G) (2, 4)
- (H) (5, 3)
- (J) (3, 5)

DIRECTIONS: Choose the best answer.

17. A rectangle has a length of 15 and width of 5. What is the perimeter?

- (A) 40
- (B) 30
- (C) 26
- (D) 24

18. Find the volume of the figure.

- (F) 36 cubic units
- (G) 30 cubic units
- (H) 32 cubic units
- (J) 35 cubic units

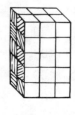

19. The load limit on a small bridge is 8 tons. What is the load limit in pounds?

  (A) 16,000 pounds

  (B) 1,600 pounds

  (C) 160 pounds

  (D) 8,000 pounds

20. Kylie ran 5 miles on Tuesday. How many feet did she run?

  (F) 500 feet

  (G) 10,000 feet

  (H) 26,400 feet

  (J) 41,250 feet

DIRECTIONS: Use the bar graph below to answer questions 21 and 22. The following information is based on the different kinds of sandwiches sold at a sandwich shop in one week.

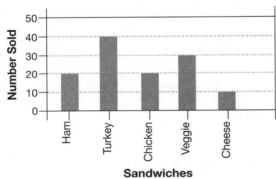

Weekly Sandwich Sales

21. How many ham sandwiches were sold during the week?

  (A) 30

  (B) 20

  (C) 10

  (D) 40

22. How many sandwiches were sold all together?

  (F) 120

  (G) 12

  (H) 100

  (J) 40

DIRECTIONS: Choose the best answer.

23. Jill bought 5 books. Each book cost $3.95. Which number sentence shows how much she paid for all 5 books?

  (A) $5 + \$3.95 = $ ▓

  (B) $5 \times \$3.95 = $ ▓

  (C) $5 - \$3.95 = $ ▓

  (D) $\$3.95 + \$3.95 = $ ▓

24. Jodi bought cans of tennis balls that cost $2.50 per can. What else do you need to know to find out how much money Jodi spent in all?

  (F) whether she played singles or doubles

  (G) how many cans of tennis balls she bought

  (H) whether she won her tennis match

  (J) how many cans of tennis balls the store had in stock

25. Ellie saved her allowance to buy a new pair of sneakers for $62.35. She had $70.00. After buying the sneakers, how much money did she have left?

  (A) $9.25

  (B) $8.75

  (C) $7.65

  (D) $6.75

26. Toby left his house for school at 7:35 A.M. He arrived at school at 7:50 A.M., which was 10 minutes before school started. How long before school started did Toby leave the house?

  (F) 10 minutes

  (G) 15 minutes

  (H) 25 minutes

  (J) 35 minutes

STOP

Final Mathematics Test
Answer Sheet

1 (A) (B) (C) (D)
2 (F) (G) (H) (J)
3 (A) (B) (C) (D)
4 (F) (G) (H) (J)
5 (A) (B) (C) (D)
6 (F) (G) (H) (J)
7 (A) (B) (C) (D)
8 (F) (G) (H) (J)
9 (A) (B) (C) (D)
10 (F) (G) (H) (J)

11 (A) (B) (C) (D)
12 (F) (G) (H) (J)
13 (A) (B) (C) (D)
14 (F) (G) (H) (J)
15 (A) (B) (C) (D)
16 (F) (G) (H) (J)
17 (A) (B) (C) (D)
18 (F) (G) (H) (J)
19 (A) (B) (C) (D)
20 (F) (G) (H) (J)

21 (A) (B) (C) (D)
22 (F) (G) (H) (J)
23 (A) (B) (C) (D)
24 (F) (G) (H) (J)
25 (A) (B) (C) (D)
26 (F) (G) (H) (J)

Social Studies Standards

Standard 1—Culture *(See pages 81–82.)*
Social studies programs should include experiences that provide for the study of culture and cultural diversity.

Standard 2—Time, Continuity, and Change *(See pages 83–84.)*
Social studies programs should include experiences that provide for the study of the way human beings view themselves in and over time.

Standard 3—People, Places, and Environments *(See pages 85–87.)*
Social studies programs should include experiences that provide for the study of people, places, and environments.

Standard 4—Individual Development and Identity *(See pages 89–90.)*
Social studies programs should include experiences that provide for the study of individual development and identity.

Standard 5—Individuals, Groups, and Institutions *(See pages 91–92.)*
Social studies programs should include experiences that provide for the study of individuals, groups, and institutions.

Standard 6—Power, Authority, and Governance *(See pages 94–95.)*
Social studies programs should include experiences that provide for the study of how people create and change structures of power, authority, and governance.

Standard 7—Production, Distribution, and Consumption *(See pages 96–97.)*
Social studies programs should include experiences that provide for the study of how people organize for the production, distribution, and consumption of goods and services.

Standard 8—Science, Technology, and Society *(See pages 98–99.)*
Social studies programs should include experiences that provide for the study of relationships among science, technology, and society.

Standard 9—Global Connections *(See pages 101–102.)*
Social studies programs should include experiences that provide for the study of global connections and interdependence.

Standard 10—Civic Ideals and Practices *(See pages 103–104.)*
Social studies programs should include experiences that provide for the study of the ideals, principles, and practices of citizenship in a democratic republic.

Social Studies

1.0

Expressions of Culture
Culture

DIRECTIONS: Choose the best answer.

Clue — **Culture** is all the things a society produces, including its arts, beliefs, and traditions. You can tell a lot about the things a society values by looking at the way the society expresses itself in its culture.

1. **Which of the following is an expression of a society's culture?**
   - (A) the movies people watch
   - (B) the clothes people wear
   - (C) the holidays people celebrate
   - (D) all of the above

2. **Christmas is a holiday celebrated by Christians around the world. In the United States, Christmas is widely observed. Schools and most businesses close on Christmas Day. People of other faiths celebrate religious holidays, too. But most schools and businesses in America do not close on those holidays. Based on this fact, which of the following do you think is most likely true?**
   - (F) Most Americans are Christians.
   - (G) Most Americans care little about religion.
   - (H) It is illegal to practice any religion besides Christianity in America.
   - (J) Most Americans are Jewish.

DIRECTIONS: Read the passage and then answer questions 3 and 4.

In Country A, poor people are expected to refer to wealthier people as "My Lord" and "My Lady." There is not much direct contact between the rich and poor. When there is, the rich are usually polite but distant toward the poor.

In Country B, poor people are not allowed to talk to wealthier people at all. The poor and the rich almost never come into contact with each other. They even celebrate completely different holidays. A rich person feels disgraced if he or she happens to touch a poor person.

In Country C, poor people and wealthy people refer to each other as "Sir" and "Ma'am." Rich and poor often attend the same schools, attend many of the same cultural events, and come into fairly frequent contact. The two groups are usually friendly to each other.

3. **Based on the above passage, which society probably places most value on ideals such as equality and fair treatment?**
   - (A) Country A
   - (B) Country B
   - (C) Country C
   - (D) All societies highly value equality and fair treatment.

4. **Based on the above passage, which society probably places most value on ideals such as tradition and keeping in your proper place?**
   - (F) Country A
   - (G) Country B
   - (H) Country C
   - (J) They all highly value such ideals.

5. **In the United States, most professional sporting events begin with the playing of the national anthem. What do you think this fact says about American society? Be as specific as you can.**

   _____

   _____

   _____

   _____

   STOP

Social Studies

| 1.0 |

Men, Women, and Children in Societies
Culture

DIRECTIONS: Read the passage. Then, answer questions 1 and 2.

In colonial times, life for the American farmer and his family was very difficult. They had to do everything that was needed for their family to survive. The primary job of the farmer was to clear the land, plant and care for the crops, take care of the animals, and maintain the property. The primary job of the farmer's wife was to take care of the family and home. This included making and washing clothes, preparing meals, tending the garden, and raising the children. The children also had chores and responsibilities. They usually started doing simple chores at a very early age. Their responsibilities increased as they got older. Some children were able to attend one-room schools. But many farming communities did not even have schools. Instead, children helped work around their farms and homes, and were taught by their parents.

1. **Based on the passage, which of the following statements is true?**

   Ⓐ The American farmer and his family made education their first priority.

   Ⓑ It required very little work to maintain a farm and home in colonial times.

   Ⓒ Every member of the family had responsibilities to do that helped the family survive.

   Ⓓ The farmer and his wife did all of the work themselves.

2. **Describe a similarity or difference you see between the children described in the passage and American children today.**

   _____

   _____

   _____

   _____

DIRECTIONS: Read the passage. Then, answer questions 3 and 4.

Ancient African societies were often organized into small groups. Each group identified itself with an important ancestor. Special respect was given to older members of the community. These tribal elders were thought of as wise and experienced. They were responsible for managing the community. They tried to be as fair to everyone as possible. Their main goal was to help the community remain peaceful and prosperous. Under this system, everyone in the community shared in the wealth as well as the hardships of their common life.

3. **Who would probably be the most respected member of an ancient African society?**

   Ⓕ a newborn baby

   Ⓖ a 20-year-old shepherd

   Ⓗ a 35-year-old pottery maker

   Ⓙ a 50-year-old tribal elder

4. **Based on the passage, most people in an ancient African community were probably _____ .**

   Ⓐ very poor, though a few were quite wealthy

   Ⓑ very wealthy, though a few were poor

   Ⓒ no better or worse off than their neighbors

   Ⓓ hostile to each other most of the time

STOP

Name _____   Date _____

2.0

Using Time Lines
Time, Continuity, and Change

DIRECTIONS: Use the following time line to answer the questions.

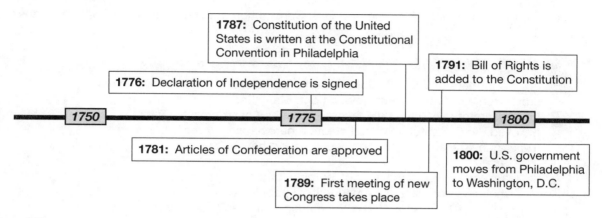

1787: Constitution of the United States is written at the Constitutional Convention in Philadelphia

1791: Bill of Rights is added to the Constitution

1776: Declaration of Independence is signed

| 1750 | 1775 | 1800 |

1781: Articles of Confederation are approved

1800: U.S. government moves from Philadelphia to Washington, D.C.

1789: First meeting of new Congress takes place

 Look at the dates in a time line carefully. Think about the order in which the events occurred.

1. **According to the time line, which event happened first?**
   - (A) The Articles of Confederation were approved.
   - (B) The Declaration of Independence was signed.
   - (C) The U.S. government moved to Washington, D.C.
   - (D) The new Congress held its first meeting.

2. **When was the Bill of Rights added to the Constitution?**
   - (F) after the U.S. government moved to Washington, D.C.
   - (G) before the first meeting of the new Congress
   - (H) before the Articles of Confederation were approved
   - (J) after the Constitution was written

3. **Which event did not occur during the 1700s?**
   - (A) the signing of the Declaration of Independence
   - (B) the writing of the Constitution
   - (C) the ratification of the Articles of Confederation
   - (D) the U.S. government move

4. **Which event occurred in the last decade of the 1700s?**
   - (F) the U.S. government move
   - (G) the signing of the Declaration of Independence
   - (H) the first meeting of the new Congress
   - (J) the addition of the Bill of Rights to the Constitution

5. **In what year did the new Congress first meet?**
   - (A) 1789
   - (B) 1798
   - (C) 1787
   - (D) 1778

Name _____ Date _____

Different Perspectives on Historical Events

Time, Continuity, and Change

DIRECTIONS: Read the following reactions to the new U.S. Constitution that was written in 1787. Then, answer the questions.

> Supporters of the U.S. Constitution were known as Federalists. They supported a strong national government. Many Federalists were wealthy. Opponents of the Constitution were known as Antifederalists. They believed the Constitution would create a national government that was too strong. They also believed it would favor the wealthy.
>
> "These lawyers, and men of learning, and moneyed men . . . make us poor illiterate [uneducated] people swallow down the pill. . . . They expect to be the manager of this Constitution, and get all the power and all the money into their own hands, and then they will swallow up all us little folks. . . . This is what I am afraid of."
>
> —Amos Singletary, farmer
>
> "I am a plain man, and get my living by the plough. . . . I did not go to any lawyer to ask his opinion; I formed my own opinion, and was pleased with this Constitution. . . . I don't think the worse of the Constitution because lawyers, and men of learning, and moneyed men, are fond of it."
>
> —Jonathan Smith, farmer
>
> Source: quotes taken from *The American Journey*, Joyce Appleby, Alan Brinkley, James M. McPherson, Glencoe/McGraw Hill, 2000, p. 212.

1. Which of these two men would be considered a Federalist? Why?

_____

_____

_____

_____

_____

_____

2. Which of these two men would be considered an Antifederalist? Why?

_____

_____

_____

_____

_____

_____

Name _____ Date _____

Social Studies

3.0

Geographic Regions of Earth
People, Places, and Environment

DIRECTIONS: Use the map below to select the best answer.

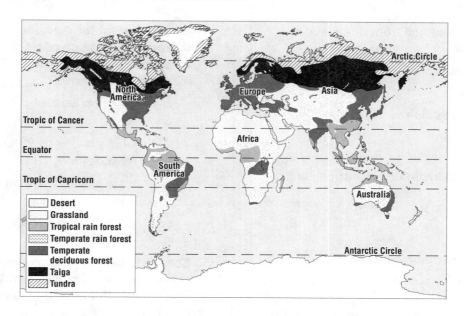

1. **Based on the map above, organisms living in the southeastern part of North America probably are most like organisms in**

   _____ .

   Ⓐ   the northern parts of Asia

   Ⓑ   most of Africa

   Ⓒ   southwestern North America

   Ⓓ   western Europe

2. **Which type of environments are found along the Equator?**

   Ⓕ   grasslands and deserts

   Ⓖ   taiga and tundra

   Ⓗ   temperate deciduous forests and deserts

   Ⓙ   tropical rain forests and grasslands

3. **The Inuit are native peoples who live in the far north. Which types of environments do the Inuit mostly live in?**

   Ⓐ   taiga and tundra

   Ⓑ   desert and grassland

   Ⓒ   taiga and temperate deciduous forest

   Ⓓ   tundra and tropical rain forest

4. **Except for Antarctica, which continent on Earth does not have any deserts?**

   Ⓕ   Australia

   Ⓖ   South America

   Ⓗ   Europe

   Ⓙ   Africa

5. **Which type of environment runs north to south in the middle section of North America?**

   Ⓐ   desert

   Ⓑ   grassland

   Ⓒ   taiga

   Ⓓ   tropical rain forest

Social Studies

3.0

Effect of Physical Processes on the Earth

People, Places, and Environment

DIRECTIONS: Select the best answer.

1. **The movement of soil from one place to another is called _____ .**

   (A) evaporation

   (B) erosion

   (C) condensation

   (D) pollution

2. **Which of the following does not cause erosion?**

   (F) wind

   (G) rain

   (H) a farmer plowing a field

   (J) all of the above cause erosion

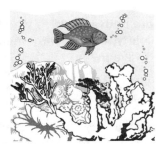

3. **Coral reefs, such as the one shown in the figure above, are formed _____ .**

   (A) over long periods of time from the shells deposited by animals

   (B) by humans who pour concrete into the water and wait for it to harden

   (C) by the gravitational pull of the sun and Moon on the Earth

   (D) quickly when low places in the land fill with rainwater

4. **During the last Ice Age, large ice sheets moved across much of Northern Europe, Asia, and North America. One result of this movement was that _____ .**

   (F) all life on Earth ended and had to start again

   (G) cities and towns throughout the world were destroyed

   (H) huge amounts of material were crushed and eventually turned into soil

   (J) Earth's first oceans were created

5. **Scientists believe that one reason the elevation of the Appalachian Mountains is much lower than the elevation of the Rocky Mountains is because _____ .**

   (A) volcanoes continually blow the tops off the Appalachians

   (B) miners chipped away most of the Appalachians when they were searching for coal

   (C) the Appalachians are much older than the Rockies, and erosion from rain has had a greater effect there

   (D) much of the Appalachians have been damaged due to overgrazing by livestock

6. **The Grand Canyon was largely formed by the effects of the _____ .**

   (F) Mississippi River

   (G) Colorado River

   (H) Ohio River

   (J) Pacific Ocean

Social Studies

3.0

Environmental Patterns
People, Places, and Environment

DIRECTIONS: Look at the diagrams below. Then, answer the questions.

Crescent Moon

Half Moon

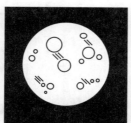
Full Moon

Half Moon

Crescent Moon

Winter

Spring

Summer

Fall

1. What do each of the diagrams above have in common?

_____

_____

_____

_____

2. Why is it important to understand that changes occur in patterns?

_____

_____

_____

_____

3. As the seasons change in your region, what types of changes take place in the weather and environment?

_____

_____

_____

_____

4. Think about the weather. If weather changes did not occur in predictable patterns, how might this change your daily life? Give an example.

_____

_____

_____

_____

STOP

Social Studies

1.0–3.0

For pages 81–87

Mini-Test 1

Culture; Time, Continuity, and Change;
People, Places, and Environment

DIRECTIONS: Choose the best answer.

1. **During the colonial period, _____ .**
   - (A) life was fairly easy for the American farmer
   - (B) most children from farming families went to school
   - (C) many children had chores and responsibilities at home
   - (D) many women worked outside the home

2. **Someone who did not support the new U.S. Constitution was known as _____ .**
   - (F) a Carpetbagger
   - (G) a Federalist
   - (H) an Antifederalist
   - (J) a patriot

Desert
Average temperature of 25°C
Average annual rainfall of less than 25 cm
Poor soil
Supports little plant life

Tropical Rain Forest
Average temperature of 25°C
Average annual rainfall of more than 300 cm
Poor soil
Supports abundant plant life

---

3. **According to the information above, what is the biggest difference between a desert and a tropical rain forest?**
   - (A) temperature
   - (B) soil
   - (C) amount of plant life supported
   - (D) amount of annual rainfall

1773:	Boston Tea Party
1775:	Battles of Lexington and Concord
1777:	British surrender at Saratoga
1783:	Treaty of Paris signed

---

4. **According to the above time line, how many years passed between the Battles of Lexington and Concord and the signing of the Treaty of Paris?**
   - (F) 2 years
   - (G) 4 years
   - (H) 6 years
   - (J) 8 years

5. **The two continents that do not have any deserts are _____ .**
   - (A) Antarctica and Africa
   - (B) Europe and Antarctica
   - (C) South America and Australia
   - (D) Asia and Europe

6. **Erosion is _____ .**
   - (F) the buildup of shells deposited by animals
   - (G) one part of the water cycle
   - (H) the movement of soil from one place to another
   - (J) the formation of soil

7. **Given a typical weather pattern, at what time of day would you expect the lowest temperature to occur?**
   - (A) noon
   - (B) 4 P.M.
   - (C) 8 P.M.
   - (D) midnight

STOP

Social Studies

| 4.0 |

Making Connections to Places
Individual Development and Identity

DIRECTIONS: Imagine that you have a new pen pal who lives in another state. Your pen pal has asked you to describe where you live. Complete the following questions about your home and community.

1. **Describe the community where you live. Do you live in the city, the suburbs, a small town, or the country? Approximately how many people live in your community? How do you travel around your community? What is something unusual or unique about your community? What do you like best about your community?**

_____

_____

_____

_____

_____

_____

_____

_____

_____

2. **Describe the home you live in. Do you live in a house, apartment, condominium, or trailer? What does it look like? What is your favorite room or space in your home? Why is it your favorite?**

_____

_____

_____

_____

_____

_____

_____

_____

STOP

Social Studies

| 4.0 |

Identifying the
Impact of Groups
Individual Development and Identity

DIRECTIONS: Think about the different groups that you are a member of, for example, you are part of a family and you are a student in a class. What other groups are you a part of in your community, school, or church? Are you on a sports team, in a choir or band, in a boys' or girls' club, or in a youth group? Pick two of these groups and write their names in the spaces below. Then, describe how being a member of these groups has affected how you live or act. Use the following questions to help you get started:

- What do I like and/or dislike about being a part of this group?
- What have I learned about others from being a part of this group?
- What have I learned about myself from being a part of this group?
- How has this group helped me become a better person?
- In what ways do I act differently since joining this group?

Group 1: _____

_____

_____

_____

_____

_____

_____

_____

Group 2: _____

_____

_____

_____

_____

_____

_____

_____

_____

STOP

Social Studies

[5.0]

Individuals, Groups, and Institutions in Society

Individuals, Groups, and Institutions

DIRECTIONS: Read the passage. Then, answer the questions.

On September 11, 2001, terrorists hijacked four American airplanes. Two of the planes crashed into the World Trade Center Towers in New York City. A third plane crashed into the Pentagon in Washington, D.C. The fourth plane crashed in a field in western Pennsylvania. Heroic passengers on this plane are believed to have fought the terrorists and prevented the plane from hitting another target. Their heroism probably saved hundreds of lives.

New York City firefighters and police officers rushed to the scene of the World Trade Center. They made a huge effort to save victims. When the towers collapsed, many firefighters and police were killed. Several thousand people who were at work in the towers were also killed or wounded.

American citizens immediately took action. Many rushed to donate blood. Doctors and nurses stood waiting outside of hospital emergency rooms. They were ready to care for the injured. Rescue workers and specially trained dogs spent days searching for survivors. Many businesses donated resources and money. Along with the American Red Cross, volunteers gave food and water to the rescue workers. U.S. citizens around the country displayed the American flag on their houses, their cars, and their clothing. They wanted to show their support for the United States. Americans felt united in the tragedy and were determined to show that such acts could not diminish American strength and pride.

1. What event happened on September 11, 2001, that caused people and institutions in America to come together?

- (A) The Vietnam War ended.
- (B) Terrorists attacked the United States.
- (C) The Gulf War began.
- (D) George W. Bush was elected president.

2. Many charitable organizations helped the victims of the September 11 tragedy. The passage identifies one in particular. Which organization was it?

- (F) the New York City Fire Department
- (G) the New York City Police Department
- (H) the American Red Cross
- (J) the Salvation Army

3. The first people who were on the scene to help at the World Trade Center were _____ .

- (A) firefighters and police
- (B) soldiers
- (C) the president and the mayor of New York City
- (D) doctors and nurses

GO

4. **How did hospitals help meet people's needs on September 11?**

   Ⓕ They sent trained dogs to help look for victims.

   Ⓖ They provided food and water to rescue workers.

   Ⓗ They took care of people injured in the attacks.

   Ⓙ They helped put out the fires at the World Trade Center.

5. **How did individual Americans help out on September 11?**

   Ⓐ They donated blood.

   Ⓑ They helped search for victims.

   Ⓒ They gave food and water to rescue workers.

   Ⓓ all of the above

6. **Following the events of September 11, many Americans displayed the U.S. flag. What did this accomplish?**

   Ⓕ It helped raise money for the victims.

   Ⓖ It helped Americans feel united and strong.

   Ⓗ It prevented the terrorists from striking again.

   Ⓙ It helped provide food for the rescue workers.

7. **Which of the institutions mentioned in the passage are run by the government and paid for by tax dollars?**

   Ⓐ the New York City Fire Department

   Ⓑ the businesses that made donations

   Ⓒ the American Red Cross

   Ⓓ the hospitals

8. **How did the passengers on one of the September 11 planes work together to accomplish something heroic?**

   _____

   _____

   _____

   _____

   _____

   _____

   _____

   _____

   _____

9. **Name at least one other group or institution not mentioned in the passage that helped on September 11, 2001. Identify the organization and explain how it helped.**

   _____

   _____

   _____

   _____

   _____

   _____

   _____

   _____

   _____

Social Studies

| 4.0–5.0 |

For pages 89–92

Mini-Test 2

Individual Development and Identity;
Individuals, Groups, and Institutions

DIRECTIONS: Think about the people who make up your immediate family, such as your dad, mom, stepparents, brothers, or sisters. Pick one of your family members and describe that person, including details such as what that family member looks like, where he or she works or goes to school, and what his or her responsibilities are at home.

1. _____

_____

_____

_____

_____

_____

_____

_____

_____

_____

2. **What is one thing you have learned from that family member about how to live or act?**

_____

_____

_____

_____

_____

_____

DIRECTIONS: Choose the best answer.

3. **Where did the planes crash during the terrorist attacks on September 11?**

   (A) New York City

   (B) Washington, D.C.

   (C) western Pennsylvania

   (D) all of the above

4. **In what year did these attacks take place?**

   (F) 2000

   (G) 2001

   (H) 2002

   (J) 2003

5. **Which of the following was not a response of the American people and institutions to these attacks?**

   (A) They worked together to rescue victims of the attacks.

   (B) Many people donated blood and many businesses donated money and resources to help with the rescue efforts.

   (C) They avoided any outward display of support for the United States.

   (D) They provided food and water to rescue workers.

STOP

Social Studies

6.0

Levels and Branches of Government

Powers, Authority, and Governance

DIRECTIONS: Choose the best answer.

1. **How many levels of government are there?**
   - (A) one
   - (B) two
   - (C) three
   - (D) four

2. **Which of the following is not one of the levels of government?**
   - (F) national
   - (G) local
   - (H) state
   - (J) judicial

3. **How many branches are at each level of the government?**
   - (A) one
   - (B) two
   - (C) three
   - (D) four

4. **Which of the following is not a branch of government?**
   - (F) executive
   - (G) legislative
   - (H) state
   - (J) judicial

5. **In the state government, who is the leader of the executive branch?**
   - (A) governor
   - (B) president
   - (C) mayor
   - (D) chief justice

6. **In the national government, which group provides the leadership for the legislative branch?**
   - (F) city council
   - (G) Congress
   - (H) State Assembly
   - (J) Supreme Court

7. **A city is one form of local government. In a city government, who is the leader of the executive branch?**
   - (A) governor
   - (B) president
   - (C) mayor
   - (D) chief justice

8. **Which branch of government is responsible for making laws?**
   - (F) executive
   - (G) legislative
   - (H) state
   - (J) judicial

9. **Which branch of government is responsible for interpreting the laws?**
   - (A) executive
   - (B) legislative
   - (C) state
   - (D) judicial

10. **Which branch of government is responsible for carrying out the laws?**
    - (F) executive
    - (G) legislative
    - (H) state
    - (J) judicial

STOP

Social Studies

6.0

Identifying Powers of the National Government

Power, Authority, and Governance

DIRECTIONS: The Articles of Confederation were written in 1777. They created the first system of government for our country. They gave most of the power to the state governments and some power to the national government. In 1787, the U.S. Constitution was written. It changed the balance of powers, creating a stronger national government. This document is the foundation for the U.S. government today. The chart below identifies which powers were given to the national government under each document. Study the chart. Then, answer the questions.

Powers of the National Government	Articles of Confederation	U.S. Constitution
Declare war	✓	✓
Print money	✓	✓
Manage foreign affairs	✓	✓
Create a postal system	✓	✓
Impose taxes		✓
Control trade with other countries		✓
Organize a court system		✓
Call state militia for service		✓
Take other necessary actions to run the government		✓

1. Which document gave the national government the power to create a postal system?

- (A) Articles of Confederation
- (B) U.S. Constitution
- (C) both of the above
- (D) none of the above

2. Which document gave the national government the power to control trade?

- (F) Articles of Confederation
- (G) U.S. Constitution
- (H) both of the above
- (J) none of the above

3. Which document gave the national government the power to declare war?

- (A) Articles of Confederation
- (B) U.S. Constitution
- (C) both of the above
- (D) none of the above

4. Which document gave the national government the power to conduct elections?

- (F) Articles of Confederation
- (G) United States Constitution
- (H) both of the above
- (J) none of the above

5. Which document gave the national government the power to organize a court system?

- (A) Articles of Confederation
- (B) U.S. Constitution
- (C) both of the above
- (D) none of the above

6. Which document gave the national government the power to impose taxes?

- (F) Articles of Confederation
- (G) U.S. Constitution
- (H) both of the above
- (J) none of the above

Social Studies

| 7.0 |

Factors Affecting Consumer Choice
Production, Distribution, and Consumption

DIRECTIONS: Choose the best answer.

1. **Suppose this week the price of hamburger goes down and the price of steak goes up. Customers visiting Fred's Meat Market today will probably _____ .**

   (A) buy more steak and less hamburger

   (B) buy the same amount of steak and more hamburger

   (C) buy less steak and more hamburger

   (D) buy less steak and less hamburger

2. **Consumers decide what to buy because of _____ .**

   (F) the quality of a product

   (G) the availability of a product

   (H) the price of a product

   (J) all of the above

DIRECTIONS: Read the story. Then, answer the questions.

On Rick's 18th birthday, he decided to buy a car. He read about all of the latest models to find the very best. After doing his research, Rick decided that he wanted a Euro 220E. The Euro 220E had lots of great features. It came with a 10-year warranty. It even had a computer and DVD player as standard equipment! This was the car for Rick.

He hurried down to the nearest Euro dealer. He was happy to see dozens of brand-new 220Es sitting in the lot. He asked to test drive one. The salesman looked at Rick and smiled. "The basic Euro 220E costs $125,000, son. Are you sure you can afford the payments?" Rick didn't say a word as he left the car lot. When he got home, he picked up the newspaper and began comparing used-car prices.

3. **Why did Rick decide not to buy the car?**

   (A) He decided at the last minute that he could find a better car.

   (B) There were not enough Euro 220Es available for everyone who wanted to buy one.

   (C) He realized that he could not afford it.

   (D) He decided it was not the right color.

4. **Economic decisions can be hard to make because we cannot have everything we want. This is called *scarcity*. Scarcity forces consumers to make choices. Which scarce resource limited Rick's choice?**

   (F) money

   (G) the number of used cars available

   (H) the number of new Euro 220Es available

   (J) all of the above

5. **Suppose one year from now Rick won $500,000 in the lottery. Would he finally be able to have his dream of owning a brand-new 220E?**

   (A) Yes, he would then have enough money to buy one.

   (B) Yes, he could afford to buy one but only if the dealership still had them on hand.

   (C) No, the salesman would remember Rick from earlier and refuse to sell it to him.

   (D) No, the salesman could not legally sell the car to Rick after refusing to sell it to him once before.

Social Studies

| 7.0 |

Supply, Demand, and Price
Production, Distribution, and Consumption

DIRECTIONS: Choose the best answer.

1. **Suppose you ran a widget factory. As the producer, at what selling price would you be most likely to produce the greatest number of them?**

   (A) $1.00

   (B) $2.50

   (C) $5.00

   (D) The same number will be sold no matter the price.

2. **Why would the producer be more likely to produce more widgets at that selling price?**

   (F) They want to sell their product at the lowest price in order to make a lower profit.

   (G) They want to sell their product at the medium price in order to break even.

   (H) They want to sell their product at the highest price in order to make a higher profit.

   (J) The selling price of the product is not their concern.

3. **Suppose you needed some widgets. At what price would you be most likely to purchase the greatest number of them?**

   (A) $1.00

   (B) $2.50

   (C) $5.00

   (D) The same number will be purchased no matter the price.

4. **When the price of something goes up, the number of people who want to buy the item usually _____ .**

   (F) goes up also

   (G) goes down

   (H) stays the same

   (J) drops to zero

5. **This fall, Danny decided to charge neighbors $5 per hour to rake their leaves. He got a few customers, but not as many as he thought he would. What would most likely happen if Danny lowered his price to $3 per hour?**

   (A) More people would decide to let Danny rake their leaves.

   (B) Danny would make a lot less money.

   (C) Danny would lose most of his customers.

   (D) His friend Alison would start raking leaves too at $5 per hour.

6. **What happens when the supply of a product goes down but the demand goes up?**

   (F) The price of the product stays the same.

   (G) The price of the product goes down.

   (H) Producers will no longer want to make the product.

   (J) The price of the product goes up.

7. **A big winter storm knocked out power to a community for several days. A local store kept several generators in stock. The generators provided a source of electricity. However, the store did not usually sell very many because they were expensive. When the storm hit the community, the store ran out of generators and had to order more. Why do you think people wanted to purchase the generators even though they were still expensive?**

   _____

   _____

   _____

   _____

STOP

Social Studies

8.0

American Inventors
Science, Technology, and Society

DIRECTIONS: Study the list of inventors and inventions/innovations below. Then, answer the questions.

Name	Invention or Innovation
Alexander Graham Bell	Telephone
John Deere	Steel plowshare
Henry Ford	Automobile assembly line
Bill Gates	Computer software
Joseph F. Glidden	Barbed wire
Thomas Edison	Electric lightbulb
John Kellogg	Cereal flakes
Samuel Morse	Telegraph
Cyrus Hall McCormick	Mechanical reaper (used to harvest crops)
Isaac Singer	Improved sewing machine

1. **Which individual is incorrectly matched with his invention or innovation?**

   (A) John Deere—steel plowshare

   (B) Joseph F. Glidden—barbed wire

   (C) John Kellogg—telegraph

   (D) Isaac Singer—sewing machine

2. **Whose invention was most responsible for freeing farmers from hours of heavy labor?**

   (F) Cyrus Hall McCormick

   (G) Alexander Graham Bell

   (H) Bill Gates

   (J) Henry Ford

3. **Which inventor created something that allowed people to talk to each other over distances?**

   (A) Joseph Glidden

   (B) Alexander Graham Bell

   (C) Bill Gates

   (D) Charles Goodyear

4. **Which inventor created something that you might have eaten for breakfast this morning?**

   (F) Alexander Graham Bell

   (G) Bill Gates

   (H) Samuel Morse

   (J) John Kellogg

5. **Which invention is used as a tool for learning in many classrooms today?**

   (A) telegraph

   (B) computer software

   (C) telephone

   (D) sewing machine

6. **How did the invention of the electric lightbulb contribute to economic change in the United States?**

   (F) Automobile factories appeared in every American city, creating jobs for millions of Americans.

   (G) It allowed travelers to move from the East Coast to the West Coast in a matter of hours, not days.

   (H) Businesses could more easily operate at night.

   (J) all of the above

7. **Henry Ford knew that he could make lots of money selling cars if he could make them cheaply. That way, many people would be able to afford to buy them. What do you think was his solution for building cars without raising their cost?**

   (A) He paid his workers only pennies a day.

   (B) He hired only friends and forced them to work long hours.

   (C) He put the people who built his cars in a line along a conveyor belt.

   (D) He built his cars with low-quality parts.

STOP

Social Studies

| 8.0 |

Protecting the Environment

Science, Technology, and Society

DIRECTIONS: Study the chart that shows how much one school has helped the environment. Then, answer the questions.

Conservation Efforts at Coe School			
Year	Pounds of Paper Recycled	Pounds of Cans Recycled	Number of Trees Planted
2004	550	475	120
2005	620	469	250
2006	685	390	320

1. **Which sentence is true about paper recycling at Coe School?**
   - (A) Students recycled more paper each year.
   - (B) Students recycled less paper each year.
   - (C) Students never recycled paper.
   - (D) Students recycled the same amount of paper each year.

2. **Which conservation project did not show better results each year?**
   - (F) recycling paper
   - (G) recycling cans
   - (H) planting trees
   - (J) They all showed better results each year.

3. **Which of the following is the most likely reason for the decrease in can recycling at Coe School?**
   - (A) Students reduced the amount of canned beverages they were drinking.
   - (B) Students found new uses for their cans.
   - (C) Students saved their cans.
   - (D) Students began recycling their cans at home.

DIRECTIONS: Choose the best answer.

4. **Which resource could be conserved by recycling a stack of newspapers?**
   - (F) rocks
   - (G) trees
   - (H) plastic
   - (J) oil

5. **Which of the following is an example of recycling to conserve resources?**
   - (A) walking to the store rather than riding in a car
   - (B) taking newspapers to a facility where they will be made into another paper product
   - (C) using a glass jelly jar as a pencil holder
   - (D) throwing aluminum cans in the trash

6. **The best example of a way to conserve natural resources is _____ .**
   - (F) regulating toxic emissions from cars
   - (G) the greenhouse effect
   - (H) cutting down on packaging used in consumer goods
   - (J) keeping garbage dumps away from residential areas

STOP

Social Studies

6.0–8.0

For pages 94–99

Mini-Test 3

Powers, Authority, and Governance; Production, Distribution, and Consumption; Science, Technology, and Society

---

DIRECTIONS: Choose the best answer.

1. **The president of the United States is the head of the executive branch of the _____ government.**
   - (A) local
   - (B) county
   - (C) state
   - (D) national

2. **The judicial branch is responsible for _____ .**
   - (F) making laws
   - (G) interpreting laws
   - (H) making sure laws are obeyed
   - (J) all of the above

3. **In what year was the U.S. Constitution written?**
   - (A) 1776
   - (B) 1777
   - (C) 1786
   - (D) 1787

4. **The power to print money was granted to the central government under which of the following documents?**
   - (F) Articles of Confederation
   - (G) United States Constitution
   - (H) both of the above
   - (J) none of the above

5. **This week the price of apples went up and the price of oranges went down. Customers shopping at the grocery store will probably _____ .**
   - (A) buy more apples and fewer oranges
   - (B) buy fewer apples and more oranges
   - (C) buy more apples and more oranges
   - (D) buy fewer apples and fewer oranges

DIRECTIONS: Read the story. Then, answer question 6.

Last holiday season, Ziffle's Department Store had 100 Dancing Danny dolls in stock. Dancing Danny dolls were in high demand last year. Ziffle's was able to charge customers $50 each for the dolls. The store sold out of Dancing Dolls in one day. This holiday season, Ziffle's ordered 500 of the dolls. Sadly, the Dancing Danny fad has passed. Very few people want the dolls this year.

6. **Which of the following will Ziffle's most likely charge for Dancing Dolls this year?**
   - (F) $100
   - (G) $75
   - (H) $50
   - (J) $25

DIRECTIONS: Choose the best answer.

7. **Assembly lines are used to manufacture products more efficiently. They were first used to manufacture which product on a large scale?**
   - (A) sewing machines
   - (B) computers
   - (C) automobiles
   - (D) jeans

8. **Trees are conserved when cardboard and newspapers are _____ .**
   - (F) taken to a dump
   - (G) burned
   - (H) kept in storage
   - (J) recycled

STOP

Name _____ Date _____

Social Studies

Global Warming
Global Connections

DIRECTIONS: Read the passage. Then, answer the questions.

Global warming refers to an increase in Earth's temperature. This change in temperature can cause changes in climate. Climate is the weather that occurs in a given place over a period of years. This includes the average weather conditions, regular weather sequences (such as seasons), and special weather events (such as hurricanes).

A warmer Earth may lead to changes in rainfall patterns and a rise in sea level. It could also have a wide range of effects on plants, wildlife, and humans. Earth has warmed by about 1°F over the past 100 years. One important contributing factor is that people do things that send greenhouse gases into the air. These gases make Earth warmer.

The Industrial Revolution took place more than 200 years ago. It was a time when people began using machines to make life easier. Before the Industrial Revolution, human activity released few gases into the atmosphere. Since then, the need for energy to run machines has continued to increase. Much of the energy we use to light and heat our homes and drive our cars comes from fossil fuels, such as coal and oil. Burning these fuels releases greenhouse gases. So whenever you watch TV, use the microwave, or ride in a car, you are sending greenhouse gases into the air. Other things can also send greenhouse gases into the air. The trash we put in landfills produces a greenhouse gas called *methane*. The animals that are raised for dairy and meat products also produce methane.

Scientists don't know for sure what effects global warming will have on Earth. The climate change could bring about health problems, such as heat stress. Climate change may also alter the world's habitats and ecosystems. If changes occur rapidly, plants and animals may not be able to react quickly enough to survive. Warmer weather could cause a rise in sea level due to melting glaciers. This could cause coastal flooding. Global warming may make Earth warmer in cold places. People living in these places might be able to grow crops in new areas. But global warming might bring drought to other places, and crops could no longer be grown. In some parts of the world, people may not have enough to eat because they cannot grow the food they need. There are still many questions about the impact of global warming. Scientists continue to study global warming in an attempt to understand its effects.

1. **Global warming affects _____ .**

   (A) Earth

   (B) our solar system

   (C) only the United States

   (D) only the northern hemisphere

2. **The weather in a given place over a period of years is called _____ .**

   (F) global warming

   (G) the climate

   (H) the greenhouse effect

   (J) seasons

GO

3. Which of the following can produce greenhouse gases that are released into the atmosphere?

    (A) coal

    (B) oil

    (C) methane

    (D) all of the above

4. Based on the passage, which of the following is not described as a potential effect of global warming?

    (F) higher temperatures

    (G) loss of species

    (H) drop in sea level

    (J) drought in some areas

5. Methane gas can be produced by _____ .

    (A) trash in landfills

    (B) burning fossil fuels

    (C) watching TV

    (D) using a microwave

6. Describe how global warming may have an impact on crops and the food supply.

_____

_____

_____

_____

_____

_____

_____

_____

_____

7. Which of the following people do you think contributes the most to global warming because of the activities they do in their daily life—a college student living in Chicago, or a mother living in a nomadic tribe in Kenya? Why?

_____

_____

_____

_____

_____

_____

_____

_____

_____

_____

_____

8. Describe five things you can do to help prevent global warming.

_____

_____

_____

_____

_____

_____

_____

_____

_____

STOP

Name _____ Date _____

Social Studies

| 10.0 |

Rights and Responsibilities of Citizens

Civic Ideals and Practices

DIRECTIONS: Choose the best answer.

1. **Every right has a responsibility that goes with it. For example, as Americans, we have the right to free speech. But this right means that we must also be sure _____ .**

   (A) never to criticize the government

   (B) to write to the president at least once every year

   (C) that the things we say are accurate and truthful

   (D) to silence any viewpoint we disagree with

2. **To be a responsible citizen, all Americans should _____ .**

   (F) obey the law

   (G) stay informed about current events

   (H) vote

   (J) all of the above

3. **In the United States, every citizen over the age of 18 has the right to vote. What are some responsibilities citizens have when it comes to voting? Explain your answer.**

   _____

   _____

   _____

   _____

   _____

4. **In the United States, if you are accused of a crime and cannot afford to hire a lawyer, the government will provide a lawyer for you. How does this benefit the accused person?**

   _____

   _____

   _____

   _____

   _____

5. **The U.S. Constitution guarantees the following rights to all U.S. citizens. Place a 1 beside the right you think is most important, a 2 beside the right you think is next important, and so on. Then, briefly explain your rankings.**

   _____ The right to keep and bear arms

   _____ The right to a speedy and public trial

   _____ The right to vote

   _____ The right to practice their religion

   _____

   _____

   _____

   _____

   _____

STOP

Social Studies

[10.0]

Natural Rights
Civic Ideals and Practices

DIRECTIONS: Read the passage. Then, complete the activity that follows.

Declaration of Independence

In 1776, the American colonists declared their independence from Great Britain in the Declaration of Independence. The document is made up of four parts. The first part is the preamble, or introduction. It explains the reasons why the colonists wanted to form a new country. The second part tells what the Americans believed were rights that all people have. The third part lists the complaints against the British King George III. The fourth part declares the colonies' independence from Britain.

The second part of the Declaration of Independence contains the following words: "We hold these truths to be self-evident [obvious], that all men are created equal, that they are endowed [given] by their Creator with certain unalienable Rights, that among these are Life, Liberty, and the pursuit of Happiness."

Clue   **Unalienable rights** are rights that cannot be taken away.

The quotation above refers to three rights—the right to life, liberty (or freedom), and the pursuit of happiness. Write a paragraph describing how these rights still apply to the lives of Americans today.

_____

_____

_____

_____

_____

_____

_____

_____

_____

_____

_____

_____

STOP

Social Studies

| 9.0–10.0 |

For pages 101–104

┌─────────────────────────┐
│   **Mini-Test 4**   │
└─────────────────────────┘

Global Connections; Civic Ideals and Practices

DIRECTIONS: Choose the best answer.

1. Global warming refers to _____ .

Ⓐ the rise in temperature during the summer

Ⓑ the winds that are produced by Earth's deserts

Ⓒ an increase in Earth's temperature

Ⓓ the melting of glaciers

2. Which of the following does not reduce greenhouse gases?

Ⓕ using solar energy to heat your home

Ⓖ recycling in order to place less trash in a landfill

Ⓗ turning off appliances when not in use

Ⓙ using a car to make short trips

3. All Americans have a constitutional right to _____ .

Ⓐ three meals per day

Ⓑ express their political opinions

Ⓒ live in a nice house

Ⓓ free health care

4. Which of the following is not an acceptable way to influence public policy?

Ⓕ Join a peaceful protest march.

Ⓖ Threaten to stop buying a company's products if it continues practices you do not like.

Ⓗ Offer to buy the mayor a new car if she votes the way you want her to on an important issue.

Ⓙ Write a letter to the editor of the local newspaper expressing your opinion.

DIRECTIONS: Read the passage. Then, answer the question.

William was a U.S. citizen. William, however, did not like many things the president and Congress were doing. He thought their actions were wrong and immoral. So, William used his computer to make a booklet that told how much he disliked the U.S. government. He printed many copies of the booklet. Then, he went downtown and gave the booklets to people he passed on the street. If someone did not want the booklet, William simply moved on to the next person.

Jane did not like what William wrote in the booklet. She asked a police officer, who was patrolling nearby, to stop William from passing out his booklets.

5. Did William and Jane respect the rights of others? Why or why not?

_____

_____

_____

_____

_____

_____

_____

_____

_____

_____

_____

_____

How Am I Doing?

Mini-Test 1

Page 88

Number Correct

7 answers correct	**Great Job!** Move on to the section test on page 108.
4–6 answers correct	**You're almost there!** But you still need a little practice. Review practice pages 81–87 before moving on to the section test on page 108.
0–3 answers correct	**Oops!** Time to review what you have learned and try again. Review the practice section on pages 81–87. Then, retake the test on page 88. Now, move on to the section test on page 108.

Mini-Test 2

Page 93

Number Correct

5 answers correct	**Awesome!** Move on to the section test on page 108.
3–4 answers correct	**You're almost there!** But you still need a little practice. Review practice pages 89–92 before moving on to the section test on page 108.
0–2 answers correct	**Oops!** Time to review what you have learned and try again. Review the practice section on pages 89–92. Then, retake the test on page 93. Now, move on to the section test on page 108.

Mini-Test 3

Page 100

Number Correct

8 answers correct	**Great Job!** Move on to the section test on page 108.
5–7 answers correct	**You're almost there!** But you still need a little practice. Review practice pages 94–99 before moving on to the section test on page 108.
0–4 answers correct	**Oops!** Time to review what you have learned and try again. Review the practice section on pages 94–99. Then, retake the test on page 100. Now, move on to the section test on page 108.

How Am I Doing?

Mini-Test 4	5 answers correct	**Awesome!** Move on to the section test on page 108.
Page 105 **Number Correct**	3–4 answers correct	**You're almost there!** But you still need a little practice. Review practice pages 101–104 before moving on to the section test on page 108.
	0–2 answers correct	**Oops!** Time to review what you have learned and try again. Review the practice section on pages 101–104. Then, retake the test on page 105. Now, move on to the section test on page 108.

Final Social Studies Test
for pages 81–105

DIRECTIONS: Choose the best answer.

1. **The holidays people celebrate are an expression of a society's _____ .**
   - (A) culture
   - (B) government
   - (C) religion
   - (D) none of the above

2. **Who was responsible for taking care of the chores on a farm during colonial times?**
   - (F) the farmer only
   - (G) the farmer and his wife
   - (H) the farmer and his children
   - (J) the farmer, his wife, and their children

DIRECTIONS: Use the information in the time line below to answer questions 2–4.

```
1783:  First hot-air balloon flight
1804:  First glider built
1900:  First flight of the Zeppelin, a rigid airship
1903:  First flight by the Wright Brothers
1957:  First artificial satellite launched
1969:  First humans land on the moon
1982:  First space shuttle mission flown
```

3. **Which event happened during the 1800s?**
   - (A) first hot-air balloon flight
   - (B) first glider built
   - (C) first artificial satellite launched
   - (D) none of the above

4. **How many years passed between the Wright Brothers' flight and the first space shuttle mission flight?**
   - (F) 79
   - (G) 82
   - (H) 66
   - (J) 97

5. **The first helicopter was flown in 1907. Where would this occur on the time line?**
   - (A) after the first Zeppelin flight and before the Wright Brothers' flight
   - (B) after the first glider was built and before the Zeppelin flight
   - (C) after the Wright Brothers' flight and before the launch of the first artificial satellite
   - (D) after the launch of the first artificial satellite and before the first humans landed on the moon

DIRECTIONS: Choose the best answer.

6. **Jaguars, toucans, and orchids live in which of the following environments?**
   - (F) desert
   - (G) grassland
   - (H) tropical rain forest
   - (J) tundra

7. **The Kabbabish are native people who herd camels through the Sahara in Africa. Which type of environment do they live in?**
   - (A) grassland
   - (B) desert
   - (C) tundra
   - (D) temperate deciduous forest

8. **The wearing away of Earth by wind, water, or glacial ice is known as _____ .**
   - (F) erosion
   - (G) flattening
   - (H) carving
   - (J) all of the above

GO

9. **Given a typical weather pattern, in which season would you experience the highest temperatures?**

   (A) spring

   (B) summer

   (C) fall

   (D) winter

10. **Which of the following provided help during and after the events on September 11, 2001?**

    (F) firefighters and police officers

    (G) hospitals

    (H) American citizens

    (J) all of the above

11. **The national government is responsible for all of the following except _____ .**

    (A) declaring war

    (B) maintaining water treatment plants

    (C) coining and printing money

    (D) maintaining a postal system

12. **The three branches of government are _____ .**

    (F) judicial, state, and executive

    (G) state, executive, and legislative

    (H) legislative, executive, and judicial

    (J) legislative, judicial, and local

13. **The Articles of Confederation gave _____ .**

    (A) the most power to state governments

    (B) the same amount of power to both the state and national governments

    (C) the most power to the national government

    (D) the most power to local governments

DIRECTIONS: Read the passage. Then, answer the questions.

The most popular snack food in years has recently hit the stores. Everyone wants to try the new Beef-o Chips. These hamburger-flavored potato chips are so popular, the manufacturer is having a hard time keeping up with the demand. Grocery stores across the nation have been mobbed by hungry customers looking to buy bags of Beef-o's. The local Food Clown store reports that an entire shelf of Beef-o's was cleaned out by customers yesterday in about five minutes.

14. **When Beef-o's first came out a couple of months ago, each bag cost $1.99. Based on the information in the passage, what do you think Beef-os might be selling for now?**

    (F) 25¢

    (G) 99¢

    (H) $1.99

    (J) $2.99

15. **Explain your answer to question 14.**

    (A) Hamburger-flavored potato chips? Yuck! Who would buy those?

    (B) When supply is high and demand is low, prices usually go down.

    (C) The price was $1.99 just a couple of months ago. That's too soon for any price change to occur.

    (D) When supply is low and demand is high, prices usually rise.

16. **Which of the following inventions helped businesses to be more productive because they could operate at night as well as during the day?**

    (F) the telephone

    (G) the electric lightbulb

    (H) the assembly line

    (J) the computer

GO

17. **Which of the following inventions did not help farmers?**

   (A) the steel plowshare

   (B) barbed wire

   (C) the telegraph

   (D) the mechanical reaper

18. **Whose use of the assembly line helped bring down the cost of making cars?**

   (F) John Deere

   (G) Henry Ford

   (H) Thomas Edison

   (J) Bill Gates

19. **Which of the following is not a benefit of conserving natural resources?**

   (A) better air quality by reducing pollutants

   (B) protecting natural areas for future generations

   (C) making fossil fuels last longer

   (D) making bigger cars

20. **Which of the following is an example of recycling to conserve resources?**

   (F) throwing tin cans in the trash

   (G) using a tin can to hold nuts and bolts

   (H) taking tin cans to a facility where they can be processed for use in steel mills

   (J) not buying food in tin cans

21. **The average increase in Earth's temperature is _____ .**

   (A) the greenhouse effect

   (B) heat stress

   (C) global warming

   (D) nothing to worry about

22. **Global warming does not affect which of the following areas?**

   (F) Antarctica

   (G) the United States

   (H) South America

   (J) all of the above are affected

23. **Burning fuels such as coal and oil releases _____ gases into the atmosphere.**

   (A) global

   (B) greenhouse

   (C) methane

   (D) warm

24. **As Americans, we have many rights. Every right, however, has a _____ that goes with it.**

   (F) consequence

   (G) test

   (H) problem

   (J) responsibility

25. **As a citizen, you have a responsibility to take part in your community. Which of the following is not a good way to do this?**

   (A) write to the president of a company protesting the treatment of women in the company's commercial

   (B) read the newspaper regularly

   (C) secretly remove books from the library that you think are unpatriotic

   (D) vote in every election

26. **The right to life, liberty, and the pursuit of happiness is given to the American people in which U.S. document?**

   (F) Articles of Confederation

   (G) Declaration of Independence

   (H) U.S. Constitution

   (J) Bill of Rights

Final Social Studies Test
Answer Sheet

1 (A) (B) (C) (D)
2 (F) (G) (H) (J)
3 (A) (B) (C) (D)
4 (F) (G) (H) (J)
5 (A) (B) (C) (D)
6 (F) (G) (H) (J)
7 (A) (B) (C) (D)
8 (F) (G) (H) (J)
9 (A) (B) (C) (D)
10 (F) (G) (H) (J)

11 (A) (B) (C) (D)
12 (F) (G) (H) (J)
13 (A) (B) (C) (D)
14 (F) (G) (H) (J)
15 (A) (B) (C) (D)
16 (F) (G) (H) (J)
17 (A) (B) (C) (D)
18 (F) (G) (H) (J)
19 (A) (B) (C) (D)
20 (F) (G) (H) (J)

21 (A) (B) (C) (D)
22 (F) (G) (H) (J)
23 (A) (B) (C) (D)
24 (F) (G) (H) (J)
25 (A) (B) (C) (D)
26 (F) (G) (H) (J)

Science Standards

Standard 1—Unifying Concepts and Processes *(See page 114.)*
As a result of the activities in grades K–12, all students should develop understanding and abilities aligned with the following concepts and processes:
- Systems, order, and organization.
- Evidence, models, and explanation.
- Constancy, change, and measurement.
- Evolution and equilibrium.
- Form and function.

Standard 2—Science as Inquiry *(See pages 115–116.)*
As a result of the activities in grades K–4, all students should develop
- The abilities necessary to do scientific inquiry.
- An understanding about scientific inquiry.

Standard 3—Physical Science *(See pages 118–120.)*
As a result of the activities in grades K–4, all students should develop an understanding of
- Properties of objects and materials.
- Position and motion of objects.
- Light, heat, electricity, and magnetism.

Standard 4—Life Science *(See pages 121–122.)*
As a result of the activities in grades K–4, all students should develop an understanding of
- Characteristics of organisms.
- Life cycles of organisms.
- Organisms and environments.

Standard 5—Earth and Space Science *(See pages 123–126.)*
As a result of the activities in grades K–4, all students should develop an understanding of
- Properties of Earth materials.
- Objects in the sky.
- Changes in Earth and sky.

Standard 6—Science and Technology *(See page 128.)*
As a result of the activities in grades K–4, all students should develop
- Abilities to distinguish between natural objects and objects made by humans.
- Abilities of technological design.
- An understanding about science and technology.

Standard 7—Science in Personal and Social Perspectives *(See page 129.)*
As a result of the activities in grades K–4, all students should develop an understanding of
- Personal health.
- Characteristics and changes in populations.
- Types of resources.
- Changes in environments.
- Science and technology in local challenges.

Science Standards

Standard 8 — History and Nature of Science *(See page 130.)*
As a result of the activities in grades K–4, all students should develop an understanding of
• Science as a human endeavor.

Name _____   Date _____

Confirming Hypotheses
Unifying Concepts and Processes

DIRECTIONS: Rebecca has been asked to research and write a report on hydropower. This topic is new to her, but she makes the hypothesis that hydropower is power that comes from water. During her research, she found the following information. Read the passage, and answer the questions that follow.

People around the world use energy every day, and some forms of energy are being used up very quickly. But resources like energy from the sun, energy from ocean waves, and hydroelectric power do not get used up completely. These resources last and last. They are called *renewable resources*. *Hydropower* is a renewable resource that is very common. The beginning of this word, *hydro*, refers to water. So, hydropower refers to power that comes from water.

What makes hydropower work? A dam looks like a tall cement wall built across a body of water. It raises the level of water in an area by blocking it. This causes the water to fall over the side of the dam. The falling water pushes against a machine called a *turbine*. The force of the falling water makes the blades inside the turbine spin. A machine called a *generator* captures the power from the spinning turbines. This makes electrical energy and sends out electricity to people who need it.

 Clue   A **hypothesis** is a guess or theory that can be tested by comparing it with observed facts.

1. **Does the passage confirm Rebecca's hypothesis? Why or why not?**

   _____

   _____

   _____

2. **What purpose does the dam serve?**
   - (A) It blocks the flow of water, raising the level of the water.
   - (B) It spins the turbines.
   - (C) It captures the power of the spinning turbines.
   - (D) It sends the electricity to the people who need it.

3. **Resources that do not run out are called** _____ .
   - (F) hydropower
   - (G) energy
   - (H) fossil fuels
   - (J) renewable resources

4. **What produces the electrical energy from the water?**
   - (A) the generator
   - (B) the turbine
   - (C) the dam
   - (D) ocean waves

Science

2.0

Scientific Inquiry
Science as Inquiry

DIRECTIONS: Choose the best answer.

Clue
- When you use **observation,** you are watching what is happening. You are not creating the event.
- When you **collect specimens,** you are collecting items to be studied.
- When you **perform an experiment,** you are actively involved in finding an answer to a question. For example, what will happen if you add baking soda to vinegar? Since the baking soda cannot add itself naturally, you must add it. Therefore, you are creating the event.

1. **Which of the following types of investigation would you use to determine the effects of using fertilizer on plants?**
   - (A) observation
   - (B) collecting specimens
   - (C) doing experiments
   - (D) all of the above

2. **Which of the following types of investigation would you use to determine how much snow is received in a given month?**
   - (F) observation
   - (G) collecting specimens
   - (H) doing experiments
   - (J) all of the above

3. **Which of the following types of investigation would you use to determine what types of fossils are contained in rocks in your area?**
   - (A) observation
   - (B) collecting specimens
   - (C) doing experiments
   - (D) all of the above

4. **Which of the following would you use to determine plants native to your area?**
   - (F) observation
   - (G) collecting specimens
   - (H) doing experiments
   - (J) all of the above

5. **A person who studies stars, planets, and space is a(n) _____ .**
   - (A) astronomer
   - (B) seismologist
   - (C) zoologist
   - (D) geologist

6. **A person who studies water and its properties is a _____ .**
   - (F) seismologist
   - (G) zoologist
   - (H) geneticist
   - (J) hydrologist

7. **A person who studies animals is a _____ .**
   - (A) geneticist
   - (B) paleontologist
   - (C) zoologist
   - (D) geologist

8. **A person who studies earthquakes is a(n) _____ .**
   - (F) seismologist
   - (G) hydrologist
   - (H) paleontologist
   - (J) astronomer

STOP

Name _____ Date _____

Scientific Results
and Knowledge
Science as Inquiry

DIRECTIONS: Read the text and then answer the question.

Similar scientific investigations seldom get the exact same results. This can be due to unexpected differences in what is being investigated or differences in the way the investigation is carried out.

Terry wanted to chart how much his flower seeds would grow in a month. In August, he planted the seeds and placed the seedlings on a windowsill that faced south. As soon as they sprouted, he carefully measured the flowers and recorded their measurements every day for the next month. Here is part of his log for the first experiment.

Day 1:	I planted the flower seedlings and placed them on a windowsill that faced south.
Day 14:	The seedlings have begun to sprout.
Day 16:	Plant One measures 1 cm; Plant Two measures 1.2 cm.
Day 44:	Plant One measures 21 cm; Plant Two measures 22 cm.

He repeated the same experiment in September, using the same location and the same flower seeds that he had used in the first experiment. Here is part of his log for the second experiment.

Day 1:	I planted the flower seedlings and placed them on a windowsill that faced south.
Day 18:	The seedlings have begun to sprout.
Day 20:	Plant One measures 0.7 cm; Plant Two measures 1 cm.
Day 48:	Plant One measures 19 cm; Plant Two measures 19.5 cm.

During the second experiment, the seeds sprouted a few days later than the seeds in the first experiment. What could have caused this?

_____

_____

_____

_____

_____

STOP

Science

| 1.0–2.0 |

For pages 114–116

Unifying Concepts and Practices; Science as Inquiry

DIRECTIONS: Choose the best answer.

1. **A guess or theory that can be tested by comparing it with observed facts is a** _____.

    Ⓐ prediction

    Ⓑ fact

    Ⓒ suggestion

    Ⓓ hypothesis

2. **Which of the following types of investigation would you use to determine what type of nest sea turtles build?**

    Ⓕ observation

    Ⓖ collecting specimens

    Ⓗ doing experiments

    Ⓙ all of the above

3. **Which of the following types of investigation would you use to determine what happens when you add hot water to ice?**

    Ⓐ observation

    Ⓑ collecting specimens

    Ⓒ doing experiments

    Ⓓ all of the above

4. **Which of the following types of investigation would you use to determine if microorganisms are found in your drinking water?**

    Ⓕ observation

    Ⓖ collecting specimens

    Ⓗ doing experiments

    Ⓙ all of the above

5. **A hydrologist is someone who studies** _____.

    Ⓐ animals

    Ⓑ stars, planets, and space

    Ⓒ water and its properties

    Ⓓ earthquakes

6. **A seismologist is someone who studies** _____.

    Ⓕ water and its properties

    Ⓖ animals

    Ⓗ earthquakes

    Ⓙ stars, planets, and space

7. **A zoologist is someone who studies** _____.

    Ⓐ insects

    Ⓑ fossils

    Ⓒ earthquakes

    Ⓓ animals

8. **JoLynn and Jon are conducting an experiment. They want to determine how many seconds it takes for a ball to hit the ground when dropped from JoLynn's one-story deck. They take turns dropping the ball and running the stopwatch. When JoLynn drops the ball, Jon records that it takes 3 seconds for it to hit the ground. When Jon drops the ball, JoLynn records that it takes 6 seconds. Why might their results have been different?**

    Ⓕ They did not drop the ball from the same height.

    Ⓖ JoLynn started the stopwatch too soon.

    Ⓗ Jon stopped the stopwatch before the ball hit the ground.

    Ⓙ Their results might have been different for all of the above reasons.

STOP

Science

3.0

Properties of Matter

Physical Science

DIRECTIONS: Choose the best answer.

1. **At which temperature would Mystery Substance X be a liquid?**

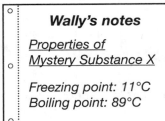

   Wally's notes

   Properties of Mystery Substance X

   Freezing point: 11°C
   Boiling point: 89°C

   Ⓐ 4°C
   Ⓑ 9°C
   Ⓒ 78°C
   Ⓓ 92°C

2. **At which temperature would Mystery Substance X be a gas?**

   Ⓕ 4°C
   Ⓖ 12°C
   Ⓗ 78°C
   Ⓙ 92°C

3. **Darion is boiling some soup in a pot. He notices that when he takes the lid off the pot, drops of water are clinging to the inside of the lid. The lid was dry when he first put it on the pot. How did the water get from the pot to the inside of the lid?**

   Ⓐ It froze there and melted.
   Ⓑ It melted and evaporated.
   Ⓒ It boiled and condensed.
   Ⓓ It melted and boiled.

4. **Physical properties of matter can be observed _____ .**

   Ⓕ without changing the matter
   Ⓖ anytime
   Ⓗ only in direct sunlight
   Ⓙ only with adult supervision

5. **Which is an example of a physical change?**

   Ⓐ metal rusting
   Ⓑ silver tarnishing
   Ⓒ water boiling
   Ⓓ paper burning

6. **Which characteristic best describes what happens during a physical change?**

   Ⓕ composition changes
   Ⓖ composition stays the same
   Ⓗ form stays the same
   Ⓙ mass is lost

7. **If matter has a fixed volume but changes its shape to fit its container, it is a _____ .**

   Ⓐ solid
   Ⓑ liquid
   Ⓒ gas
   Ⓓ suspension

8. **Steam is water in its _____ state.**

   Ⓕ solid
   Ⓖ changing
   Ⓗ liquid
   Ⓙ gas

STOP

Science
3.0

Types of Motion

Physical Science

DIRECTIONS: Read each type of motion described below. If the motion of the object being described is constant, write a **C** in the space provided. If the motion is variable, write a **V** in the space provided. If the motion is periodic, write a **P** in the space provided.

Clue

Constant motion means it is a continuous and nonstop type of motion. **Variable** motion means the motion can change at any time. **Periodic** motion means the motion occurs at regular or predictable periods of time.

_____ 1. The pendulum of a grandfather clock moves back and forth one beat per second.

_____ 2. A toy car travels five feet, hits a wall, bounces off it and turns in another direction, then travels another five feet.

_____ 3. A bowling ball rolls down the alley.

_____ 4. Earth rotates around the sun.

_____ 5. A baseball is thrown from the pitcher and caught by the catcher.

_____ 6. A baseball is thrown from the pitcher, hit by the batter on the ground to the shortstop, and picked up by the shortstop and thrown to first base.

_____ 7. Your heart beats regularly as you sit quietly and read a book.

_____ 8. A truck travels on an Interstate highway for 40 miles at 55 miles per hour.

_____ 9. A truck travels down Main Street for one block at 25 miles per hour, slows to a stop at a red light, turns left onto Third Avenue, and slowly reaches a speed of 15 miles per hour before stopping again at another red light.

_____ 10. The minute hand on your clock moves from 9:01 to 9:02.

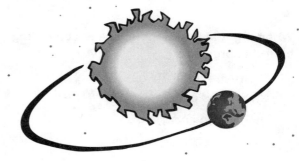

STOP

Science

3.0

Forms of Energy

Physical Science

DIRECTIONS: Choose the best answer.

1. When an object has stored energy, it is waiting to do work. Stored energy is called _____ .
   - (A) sound energy
   - (B) potential energy
   - (C) kinetic energy
   - (D) inactive energy

2. When an object has active energy, it is moving. Active energy is called _____ .
   - (F) sound energy
   - (G) potential energy
   - (H) kinetic energy
   - (J) inactive energy

3. The word *kinetic* relates to _____ .
   - (A) the amount of matter in an object
   - (B) motion
   - (C) the attractive force between two objects
   - (D) the measurement of force

4. When a girl starts running, she is converting stored energy into _____ .
   - (F) nuclear energy
   - (G) sound energy
   - (H) kinetic energy
   - (J) light energy

5. Which of the following is not a form of energy?
   - (A) liquid
   - (B) heat
   - (C) light
   - (D) chemical

6. Temperature is a measure of what form of energy?
   - (F) electric
   - (G) heat
   - (H) light
   - (J) nuclear

7. Heat and sound travel in _____ .
   - (A) beams
   - (B) drops
   - (C) waves
   - (D) currents

8. What is the name of the energy from the sun?
   - (F) solar
   - (G) polar
   - (H) ocular
   - (J) lunar

9. The transfer of heat between two objects that touch is called _____ .
   - (A) radiation
   - (B) convection
   - (C) conduction
   - (D) condensation

10. In a lightbulb, electrical energy is converted to light and _____ energy.
   - (F) mechanical
   - (G) solar
   - (H) heat
   - (J) chemical

Science
4.0

Organisms in Ecosystems

Life Science

DIRECTIONS: Choose the best answer.

1. **The place where an organism lives is its _____ .**
   - (A) habitat
   - (B) community
   - (C) niche
   - (D) ecosystem

2. **All of the living organisms within an area form a(n) _____ .**
   - (F) niche
   - (G) ecosystem
   - (H) habitat
   - (J) community

3. **The unique role of an organism in the community is its _____ .**
   - (A) ecosystem
   - (B) habitat
   - (C) niche
   - (D) none of the above

4. **A community of plants and animals that interact together in an environment is called a(n) _____ .**
   - (F) habitat
   - (G) niche
   - (H) ecosystem
   - (J) none of the above

5. **Some organisms have special adaptations that help them blend into the background of their environment so that predators cannot see them. This is called _____ .**
   - (A) blendability
   - (B) camouflage
   - (C) selection
   - (D) fusion

6. **An organism that lives by feeding on other organisms is called a _____ .**
   - (F) producer
   - (G) consumer
   - (H) decomposer
   - (J) none of the above

7. **An organism, usually a green plant, that can make its own food is called a _____ .**
   - (A) consumer
   - (B) decomposer
   - (C) producer
   - (D) none of the above

8. **An organism that feeds on the remains of other organisms is called a _____ .**
   - (F) decomposer
   - (G) producer
   - (H) consumer
   - (J) none of the above

STOP

Name _____ Date _____

Factors Affecting
Life Spans/Life Cycles
Life Science

DIRECTIONS: Choose the best answer.

1. **Assuming that there are no predators, which of the following does not affect the size of an animal population?**

    (A) the amount of water available

    (B) the amount of plants or other food source available

    (C) the amount of space available

    (D) the number of hiding places available

2. **In a predator-prey relationship, when the predator population increases, the prey population will probably _____ .**

    (F) increase

    (G) decrease

    (H) stay the same

    (J) not enough information to know

3. **In a predator-prey relationship, when the prey population increases, the predator population will probably _____ .**

    (A) increase

    (B) decrease

    (C) stay the same

    (D) not enough information to know

4. **Which of the following is most likely to have a shorter life span if rainfall is well above normal?**

    (F) ivy

    (G) cactus

    (H) seal

    (J) redwood tree

5. **If the temperature in a warm region, such as a desert, suddenly dropped by 50 degrees, what types of organisms might completely die out?**

    _____

    _____

    _____

    _____

    _____

6. **Which organisms would thrive in a colder environment? What challenges might they still face?**

    _____

    _____

    _____

    _____

    _____

7. **What would change if the climate suddenly became 50 degrees warmer?**

    _____

    _____

    _____

    _____

    _____

    _____

Science

5.0

Patterns in the Solar System

Earth and Space Science

DIRECTIONS: Read the selection. Then, choose the best answer.

Why Are There Seasons?

Earth revolves around the sun. It also spins on an invisible axis that runs through its center.

It takes $365\frac{1}{4}$ days, or one year, for Earth to revolve once around the Sun. Just as the Moon moves in an orbit around Earth, Earth moves around the sun. Earth does not move in a perfect circle. Its orbit is an ellipse, which is a flattened circle, like an oval. As Earth revolves around the sun in an elliptical shape, it spins on its invisible axis.

Earth's axis of rotation is not straight up and down; it is tilted. This important feature produces the seasons on Earth. No matter where Earth is in its rotation around the sun, its axis is tilted in the same direction and at the same angle. So, as Earth moves, different parts of it are facing the sun and different parts are facing away. The North Pole is tilting toward the sun in June, so the northern half of Earth is enjoying summer. In December, the North Pole is tilted away from the sun, so the northern part of the world experiences winter.

This important relationship between Earth and the sun determines how hot and cold we are, when we plant our crops, and whether we have droughts or floods.

1. **If North America is having summer, what season would the Australians be having?**

   (A) spring

   (B) summer

   (C) winter

   (D) fall

2. **What would happen if Earth's axis were not tilted, but straight up and down?**

   (F) Nothing would change.

   (G) Earth wouldn't change seasons.

   (H) It would always be summer on Earth.

   (J) It would always be winter on Earth.

3. **Based on the passage, which of the following statements is not true?**

   (A) Earth moves around the sun in an elliptical orbit.

   (B) When the North Pole is tilting toward the sun, it is summer in the Northern Hemisphere.

   (C) Earth revolves around the sun every six months.

   (D) Earth is always tilted in the same direction and at the same angle.

DIRECTIONS: Choose the best answer.

4. **Patterns made by stars in the night sky are called _____ .**

   (F) constellations

   (G) galaxies

   (H) nebulas

   (J) comets

5. **Study the chart below and determine what the moon phase will be during week 6.**

(A)   (C)

(B)   (D)

STOP

Science

5.0

Properties of Water

Earth and Space Science

DIRECTIONS: Choose the best answer.

1. Ice is water in its _____ state.
   - (A) solid
   - (B) changing
   - (C) liquid
   - (D) gas

2. When water freezes, it changes from a _____ .
   - (F) gas to a solid
   - (G) liquid to a gas
   - (H) liquid to a solid
   - (J) solid to a gas

3. Malcom left a cube of ice in a glass on a window sill. In about an hour, the ice changed into a clear substance that took on the shape of the lower part of the glass. Finally, after three days, there appeared to be nothing in the glass at all. What states of matter did the ice cube pass through?
   - (A) liquid then gas then solid
   - (B) solid then liquid then gas
   - (C) gas then liquid then solid
   - (D) solid then gas then liquid

4. At which temperature does water become a solid?
   - (F) 32°C
   - (H) 32°F
   - (G) 0°F
   - (J) 100°C

5. The water cycle occurs between Earth and the _____ .
   - (A) hydrosphere
   - (B) atmosphere
   - (C) stratosphere
   - (D) biosphere

6. Which of the following has the least effect on the water cycle?
   - (F) temperature
   - (G) air pressure
   - (H) land features
   - (J) soil

7. Water vapor forming droplets that form clouds directly involves which process?
   - (A) condensation
   - (B) precipitation
   - (C) evaporation
   - (D) transpiration

8. In the water cycle, how is water returned to the atmosphere?
   - (F) evaporation
   - (G) condensation
   - (H) precipitation
   - (J) fixation

9. A rainstorm is an example of _____ .
   - (A) precipitation
   - (B) evaporation
   - (C) condensation
   - (D) respiration

10. When a puddle of water disappears after the sun comes out, it is called _____ .
    - (F) precipitation
    - (G) transpiration
    - (H) condensation
    - (J) evaporation

STOP

Science
5.0

Weather

Earth and Space Science

DIRECTIONS: Choose the best answer.

1. **Which of the following instruments would you use to determine how fast the wind is blowing?**
   - (A) a wind vane
   - (B) a barometer
   - (C) an anemometer
   - (D) a thermometer

2. **Which of the following instruments would you use to measure air pressure?**
   - (F) an anemometer
   - (G) a wind vane
   - (H) a thermometer
   - (J) a barometer

3. **What does a rain gauge measure?**
   - (A) the amount of rainfall
   - (B) the intensity of rainfall
   - (C) the anticipated rainfall
   - (D) how long the rain falls

4. **A cold front on a weather map is indicated by _____ .**
   - (F) a blue line with triangles pointing in the direction that the cold air is moving
   - (G) a blue line with semicircles pointing in the direction that the cold air is moving
   - (H) a red line with triangles pointing in the direction that the cold air is moving
   - (J) a red line with semicircles pointing in the direction that the cold air is moving

5. **Warm, low-pressure air can hold more water than cold air. As warm air rises, it cools. This causes water vapor to gather together, or condense, into water drops. What kind of weather probably goes along with low air pressure?**
   - (A) clouds and rain
   - (B) clouds without rain
   - (C) clear skies
   - (D) tornadoes

6. **Climate is different from weather in that it _____ .**
   - (F) changes more rapidly
   - (G) changes less rapidly
   - (H) is more extreme
   - (J) is reported daily on local television news

7. **Study the table below. Which month is likely to have the most hurricanes?**
   - (A) July
   - (B) August
   - (C) September
   - (D) October

Month Formed	Tropical Storms	Hurricanes
January–April	4	1
May	14	3
June	57	23
July	68	35
August	221	?
September	311	?
October	188	?
November	42	22
December	6	3

STOP

Science
5.0

Earth's Processes
Earth and Space Science

DIRECTIONS: Choose the best answer.

1. What is a mixture of weathered rock and organic matter called?
   - (A) soil
   - (B) limestone
   - (C) carbon dioxide
   - (D) clay

2. What is another term for decayed organic matter found in soil?
   - (F) leaching
   - (G) humus
   - (H) soil
   - (J) sediment

3. What occurs when weathered rock and organic matter are mixed together?
   - (A) leaching
   - (B) oxidation
   - (C) soil erosion
   - (D) soil formation

4. What type of wind erosion moves small sediments but leaves pebbles and boulders behind?
   - (F) deflation
   - (G) loess
   - (H) abrasion
   - (J) sandblasting

5. Which of the following is the slowest type of mass movement?
   - (A) abrasion
   - (B) creep
   - (C) slump
   - (D) mudflow

6. A large mass of material, such as snow, mud, or rock, falling or sliding rapidly under the force of gravity is a(n) _____ .
   - (F) volcano
   - (G) tsunami
   - (H) earthquake
   - (J) avalanche

7. Movement along a fault line in Earth's crust is the cause of which of the following?
   - (A) a flood
   - (B) an earthquake
   - (C) a volcanic eruption
   - (D) a tornado

8. Liquid rock, or magma, that reaches Earth's surface is called _____ .
   - (F) ash
   - (G) coral
   - (H) lava
   - (J) fossil

9. A great wave that starts in the ocean because of a sudden disturbance in the ocean floor is known as a(n) _____ .
   - (A) tsunami
   - (B) avalanche
   - (C) hurricane
   - (D) flood

10. Which of the following causes a volcano to erupt?
    - (F) The temperature in Earth's core.
    - (G) The temperature on Earth's surface.
    - (H) Gas pressure builds up within Earth.
    - (J) all of the above

STOP

Science

3.0–5.0

For pages 118–126

Mini-Test 2

Physical Science; Life Science; Earth and Space Science

DIRECTIONS: Choose the best answer.

1. **Jerome wanted to make breakfast. First, he cracked several eggs into a bowl and stirred them briskly. Second, he grated low-fat cheese into the bowl. Third, he ground fresh black pepper into the bowl. After stirring the contents of the bowl, Jerome emptied it into a hot skillet and cooked the ingredients to perfection. Which of the steps is not a physical change?**

   (A) cracking eggs into a bowl

   (B) grating the cheese

   (C) grinding the black pepper

   (D) cooking the eggs

2. **Which of the following is not a form of energy?**

   (F) solar

   (G) solid

   (H) electrical

   (J) kinetic

3. **In a predator-prey relationship, when the predator population decreases, the prey population will probably _____ .**

   (A) increase

   (B) decrease

   (C) stay the same

   (D) not enough information to know

4. **Which of the following is an example of a producer?**

   (F) cactus

   (G) lion

   (H) bacteria

   (J) trout

5. **Which of the following is an example of a decomposer?**

   (A) cactus

   (B) lion

   (C) bacteria

   (D) trout

6. **One morning, you wake up and find dew on the yard. Throughout the day, the weather is hot and sunny. Later that day, you notice that the dew is gone. This is an example of _____ .**

   (F) condensation

   (G) evaporation

   (H) precipitation

   (J) transpiration

7. **In the water cycle, how does water reach Earth?**

   (A) condensation

   (B) evaporation

   (C) precipitation

   (D) transpiration

8. **How long does it take for Earth to complete one rotation on its axis?**

   (F) one hour

   (G) one day

   (H) one week

   (J) one month

9. **Which of the following instruments tells you in which direction the wind is blowing?**

   (A) an anemometer

   (B) a barometer

   (C) a wind vane

   (D) a thermometer

STOP

Use of Technology in Science

Science

6.0

Science and Technology

DIRECTIONS: Choose the best answer.

1. **Which of the following would you use to study organisms in a drop of water?**

   Ⓐ a telescope

   Ⓑ a microscope

   Ⓒ a magnifying glass

   Ⓓ a bifocal lens

2. **Which of the following would you use to determine which runs faster—a dog or a cat?**

   Ⓕ a ruler

   Ⓖ a stopwatch

   Ⓗ a barometer

   Ⓙ an odometer

3. **Which of the following would you use to determine if a solution is an acid or a base?**

   Ⓐ litmus paper

   Ⓑ construction paper

   Ⓒ a microscope

   Ⓓ a telescope

4. **Which instrument would a scientist use to measure the speed of a falling object?**

   Ⓕ a stopwatch

   Ⓖ a microscope

   Ⓗ a balance scale

   Ⓙ a ruler

5. **What tool would a scientist use to measure liquids in a laboratory?**

   Ⓐ a graduated cylinder

   Ⓑ a beaker

   Ⓒ a Petri dish

   Ⓓ a scalpel

6. **Describe one way a scientist might use technology to communicate the findings of an experiment to other scientists.**

   _____

   _____

   _____

   _____

   _____

   _____

7. **Describe one way technology has made it easier for scientists to help people stay healthy.**

   _____

   _____

   _____

   _____

   _____

   _____

STOP

Science
7.0

Nutrition and Exercise

Science in Personal and Social Perspectives

DIRECTIONS: Study the food pyramid. Each triangle in the pyramid shows how much you should eat from that food group every day in relation to the other food groups. Then, answer the questions.

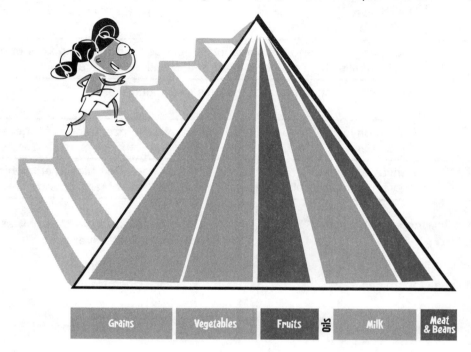

Grains   Vegetables   Fruits   Oils   Milk   Meat & Beans

1. **From which of the following food groups should you eat the most daily servings?**
   - (A) grains
   - (B) vegetables
   - (C) fruits
   - (D) meat and beans

2. **From which of the following food groups should you eat the fewest daily servings?**
   - (F) vegetables
   - (G) milk
   - (H) meat and beans
   - (J) grains

3. **What food is a substitute for meat?**
   - (A) oils
   - (B) fruits
   - (C) vegetables
   - (D) beans

4. **What does the staircase represent?**
   - (F) You should be physically active every day.
   - (G) You should run before eating.
   - (H) You should climb stairs every day.
   - (J) You should race others to finish eating.

5. **Which of the following is not a food group?**
   - (A) milk
   - (B) fruits
   - (C) candy
   - (D) beans

6. **Which of the following is not part of the meat and beans food group?**
   - (F) fish
   - (G) peanuts
   - (H) chicken
   - (J) yogurt

STOP

Science
8.0

Famous Scientists

History and Nature of Science

DIRECTIONS: Study the chart below. Then, choose the best answer.

Nicholaus Copernicus 1473–1543	Polish astronomer; famous for the theories that Earth is a moving planet and the sun is the center of the universe
Isaac Newton 1642–1727	English physicist and mathematician; famous for developing laws of motion and gravity as well as a new branch of mathematics known as *calculus*
Charles Darwin 1809–1882	British naturalist; famous for theories of evolution
Marie Curie 1867–1934	French physicist; first woman to win the Nobel Prize; famous for her research on radioactivity
Wangari Maathai 1940–	Kenyan scientist; famous for founding the Green Belt Movement, which encouraged Kenyan women to plant trees to prevent soil erosion and provide firewood

1. Which of the following scientists was a mathematician?

- (A) Marie Curie
- (B) Nicholaus Copernicus
- (C) Isaac Newton
- (D) Wangari Maathai

2. Who developed theories of evolution?

- (F) Charles Darwin
- (G) Marie Curie
- (H) Wangari Maathai
- (J) Isaac Newton

3. Which of the following scientists made the earliest discoveries?

- (A) Isaac Newton
- (B) Wangari Maathai
- (C) Charles Darwin
- (D) Nicholaus Copernicus

4. Which of the following scientists was a physicist?

- (F) Isaac Newton
- (G) Nicholaus Copernicus
- (H) Marie Curie
- (J) both F and H

5. Who developed the theory that the sun is the center of the universe?

- (A) Charles Darwin
- (B) Isaac Newton
- (C) Marie Curie
- (D) Nicholaus Copernicus

6. Who became famous for work on preventing soil erosion?

- (F) Wangari Maathai
- (G) Marie Curie
- (H) Charles Darwin
- (J) Isaac Newton

7. Who researched radioactivity?

- (A) Marie Curie
- (B) Nicholaus Copernicus
- (C) Isaac Newton
- (D) Wangari Maathai

8. Who developed a new branch of mathematics called *calculus?*

- (F) Wangari Maathai
- (G) Marie Curie
- (H) Charles Darwin
- (J) Isaac Newton

Science

6.0–8.0

For pages 128–130

Mini-Test 3

Science and Technology; Science in Personal and Social Perspectives; History and Nature of Science

DIRECTIONS: Choose the best answer.

1. **Which instrument is used to examine the features of the Moon?**

   Ⓐ stethoscope

   Ⓑ microscope

   Ⓒ thermometer

   Ⓓ telescope

2. **Which instrument is used to listen to a person's heart?**

   Ⓕ stethoscope

   Ⓖ gyroscope

   Ⓗ telescope

   Ⓙ endoscope

3. **Which instrument is used to view the cells in a drop of blood?**

   Ⓐ telescope

   Ⓑ microscope

   Ⓒ magnifying glass

   Ⓓ stethoscope

4. **Which of the following is not part of the grains food group?**

   Ⓕ oatmeal

   Ⓖ rice

   Ⓗ bread

   Ⓙ peanuts

5. **Which of the following is not part of the milk food group?**

   Ⓐ yogurt

   Ⓑ rice

   Ⓒ ice cream

   Ⓓ cheese

6. **How many food groups are included on the food pyramid?**

   Ⓕ 4

   Ⓖ 5

   Ⓗ 6

   Ⓙ 7

7. **Which scientist is known for developing laws of motion and gravity?**

   Ⓐ Charles Darwin

   Ⓑ Isaac Newton

   Ⓒ Marie Curie

   Ⓓ Nicholaus Copernicus

8. **Charles Darwin was a British _____ .**

   Ⓕ astronomer

   Ⓖ physicist

   Ⓗ mathematician

   Ⓙ naturalist

9. **Which scientist is known for founding the Green Belt Movement?**

   Ⓐ Marie Curie

   Ⓑ Wangari Maathai

   Ⓒ Isaac Newton

   Ⓓ Nicholaus Copernicus

10. **Isaac Newton and Marie Curie were both _____ .**

   Ⓕ physicists

   Ⓖ astronomers

   Ⓗ naturalists

   Ⓙ mathematicians

STOP

How Am I Doing?

Mini-Test 1 Page 117 **Number Correct**	**8** answers correct	**Great Job!** Move on to the section test on page 133.
	5–7 answers correct	**You're almost there!** But you still need a little practice. Review practice pages 114–116 before moving on to the section test on page 133.
	0–4 answers correct	**Oops!** Time to review what you have learned and try again. Review the practice section on pages 114–116. Then, retake the test on page 117. Now, move on to the section test on page 133.
Mini-Test 2 Page 127 **Number Correct**	**9** answers correct	**Awesome!** Move on to the section test on page 133.
	5–8 answers correct	**You're almost there!** But you still need a little practice. Review practice pages 118–126 before moving on to the section test on page 133.
	0–4 answers correct	**Oops!** Time to review what you have learned and try again. Review the practice section on pages 118–126. Then, retake the test on page 127. Now, move on to the section test on page 133.
Mini-Test 3 Page 131 **Number Correct**	**9–10** answers correct	**Great Job!** Move on to the section test on page 133.
	5–8 answers correct	**You're almost there!** But you still need a little practice. Review practice pages 128–130 before moving on to the section test on page 133.
	0–4 answers correct	**Oops!** Time to review what you have learned and try again. Review the practice section on pages 128–130. Then, retake the test on page 131. Now, move on to the section test on page 133.

Name _____ Date _____

Final Science Test
For pages 114–131

DIRECTIONS: Choose the best answer.

1. Jan read an article about how the dinosaurs became extinct. It said that most scientists agreed that at some time in the past a huge asteroid had hit Earth. This caused certain environmental changes that made it difficult for dinosaurs to survive. Scientists have several hypotheses about how the asteroid killed off the dinosaurs. Which of the following seems most likely?
   - (A) It caused an ice age.
   - (B) It caused fires that destroyed food dinosaurs needed to survive.
   - (C) It caused "space sickness."
   - (D) It turned the dinosaurs to stone.

2. Which of the following types of investigation would you use to determine the effects of sunlight versus artificial light on plants?
   - (F) observation
   - (G) collecting specimens
   - (H) doing experiments
   - (J) all of the above

3. What does an astronomer study?
   - (A) plants
   - (B) stars, planets, and space
   - (C) fossils and rocks
   - (D) cells

4. A person who studies microscopic plants and animals is a _____ .
   - (F) geologist
   - (G) hydrologist
   - (H) zoologist
   - (J) microbiologist

5. When water melts from an ice cube, it is an example of a physical change. The water changes from a _____ .
   - (A) solid to a gas
   - (B) liquid to a vapor
   - (C) solid to a liquid
   - (D) liquid to a solid

6. How can you change matter from one state to another?
   - (F) by changing its container
   - (G) by adding or removing heat
   - (H) by dividing it in half
   - (J) by changing its volume

7. In a battery, chemical energy changes to _____ .
   - (A) electrical energy
   - (B) solar energy
   - (C) heat energy
   - (D) light energy

8. _____ is the measure of heat or thermal energy.
   - (F) Mass
   - (G) Density
   - (H) Temperature
   - (D) Force

9. Motion that can change at any time is called _____ motion.
   - (A) constant
   - (B) variable
   - (C) periodic
   - (D) sudden

GO

10. A palm tree is an example of a _____ .

   (F) producer

   (G) consumer

   (H) decomposer

   (J) community

11. A decomposer is an organism that _____ .

   (A) lives by feeding on other organisms

   (B) feeds on the remains of other organisms

   (C) makes its own food

   (D) none of the above

12. What is made up of all living organisms in an area?

   (F) niche

   (G) habitat

   (H) community

   (J) ecosystem

13. Which of the following is likely to have a shorter life span if rainfall decreases?

   (A) cactus

   (B) camel

   (C) whale

   (D) fern

14. A trait or ability that helps an organism survive in its environment is called a(n) _____ .

   (F) response

   (G) adaptation

   (H) ecosystem

   (D) organization

15. Study the chart below. What will the moon phase probably be on March 26?

Date	Moon Phase
December 29	Full moon
January 5	Last quarter
January 11	New moon
January 19	First quarter
January 27	Full moon
February 3	Last quarter
February 10	New moon
February 18	First quarter
February 26	Full moon

   (A) full moon

   (B) last quarter

   (C) new moon

   (D) first quarter

16. How long does it take for Earth to revolve around the sun?

   (F) one day

   (G) one week

   (H) one month

   (J) one year

17. Study the table below. Predict which season the southern hemisphere will have during the month of September.

Month	Northern Hemisphere	Southern Hemisphere
December	Winter	Summer
March	Spring	Autumn
June	Summer	Winter
September	Autumn	?

   (A) Autumn

   (B) Winter

   (C) Summer

   (D) Spring

GO

18. Which of the following is not part of the water cycle?

   (F) evaporation

   (G) condensation

   (H) precipitation

   (J) respiration

19. Which of the following is a form of precipitation?

   (A) rain

   (B) snow

   (C) sleet

   (D) all of the above

20. What does a barometer measure?

   (F) wind speed

   (G) temperature

   (H) air pressure

   (J) wind direction

21. On a weather map, a red line with semicircles indicates _____ .

   (A) a cold front

   (B) a warm front

   (C) low air pressure

   (D) high air pressure

22. A weather front passed through the state of Georgia today. Low-pressure air moved off to the east and was replaced by high-pressure air from the west. What kind of weather is most likely to occur in Georgia tomorrow?

   (F) thunderstorms

   (G) clear, cooler, and sunny

   (H) warmer and mostly cloudy

   (J) snow

23. Liquid rock found inside volcanoes is known as _____ .

   (A) magma

   (B) fossil

   (C) igneous rock

   (D) ash

24. Which of the following would you use to record the speed of various falling objects?

   (F) a clock with minute and hour hands

   (G) an anemometer

   (H) a stopwatch

   (J) an hourglass

25. What is represented in the food pyramid diagram in addition to the food groups?

   (A) learning

   (B) physical activity

   (C) sleep

   (D) calories

26. The width of the stripes in the food pyramid diagram represent which of the following?

   (F) the number of calories in the food groups

   (G) the number of daily servings you should eat from the food groups

   (H) the variety of foods within the food groups

   (J) the widths have no meaning

27. Isaac Newton is known for _____ .

   (A) developing theories that Earth is a moving planet

   (B) researching radioactivity

   (C) developing theories of evolution

   (D) developing laws of motion and gravity

STOP

Name _____ Date _____

Final Science Test
Answer Sheet

1 (A) (B) (C) (D)
2 (F) (G) (H) (J)
3 (A) (B) (C) (D)
4 (F) (G) (H) (J)
5 (A) (B) (C) (D)
6 (F) (G) (H) (J)
7 (A) (B) (C) (D)
8 (F) (G) (H) (J)
9 (A) (B) (C) (D)
10 (F) (G) (H) (J)

11 (A) (B) (C) (D)
12 (F) (G) (H) (J)
13 (A) (B) (C) (D)
14 (F) (G) (H) (J)
15 (A) (B) (C) (D)
16 (F) (G) (H) (J)
17 (A) (B) (C) (D)
18 (F) (G) (H) (J)
19 (A) (B) (C) (D)
20 (F) (G) (H) (J)

21 (A) (B) (C) (D)
22 (F) (G) (H) (J)
23 (A) (B) (C) (D)
24 (F) (G) (H) (J)
25 (A) (B) (C) (D)
26 (F) (G) (H) (J)
27 (A) (B) (C) (D)

Answer Key

Page 9
1. fiction
2. a problem
3. the mother
4. *Mom to the Rescue*
5. A

Page 10
1. B
2. H
3. D
4. Students should explain which words or phrases in the story helped them figure out the setting. For example, after they started going down the hill so fast; twist, a loop, fast turns, everyone screamed in delight

Page 11
1. Students should mention the origin of the telegraph.
2. Students should cite details from the reading selection, such as Morse's inspiration on the ship and the stages of development of his invention (1835, 1844, and 1849).
3. C
4. H

Pages 12–13
1. C
2. The passage is about Jacqueline Cochran's life.
3. J
4. The story is about an animal and has a moral.
5. B
6. The passage is set up in lines and has rhyming words.

Page 14
1. Answers will vary. The narrator likes the family tradition, but some students might say that the narrator hints that he or she might like more of his or her own gifts.
2. Maggie hugged her stuffed animal and looked at the narrator.
3. because it is not like a traditional birthday
4. Yes, because the narrator seems to enjoy the happiness the tradition brings to others.

Page 15
1. D
2. G
3. A
4. G

Page 16
1. C
2. F
3. D
4. H

Page 17
1. B
2. G
3. D
4. H
5. A
6. H
7. B
8. F

Page 18 Mini-Test 1
1. C
2. G
3. C
4. G

Page 19
1. A
2. J
3. C
4. H
5. A
6. F
7. C
8. H
9. A
10. J

Page 20
1. S
2. F
3. S
4. F
5. F
6. S
7. S
8. S
9. F
10. S
11. B
12. J
13. and

14. but
15. or
16. but
17. and
18. but
19. or

Page 21
1. DE
2. DE
3. IN
4. EX
5. IM
6. DE
7. IM
8. IN
9. EX
10. DE
11. IN
12. IM
13. DE
14. EX
15. IN
16. IM

Page 22
1. C
2. F
3. Answers will vary. Students should note that the outline gives Kyle a plan to follow for his report. He can use the outline to organize his information in a logical order. It will help make it easier to write his drafts.

Page 23
1. Hannah's family car has broken down in the middle of the desert.

2. Answers will vary but students should give two possible endings to the story.

3. Answers will vary, but students should list sights, sounds, and feelings that someone would experience in this situation. Example: very little sound, miles and miles of sand, getting hot and hungry, and perhaps fear.

4. Students should write an ending to this story.

Page 24
1. Answers will vary. Students should list the title of a book or movie they enjoyed.

2. Students should give reasons why others might enjoy reading the book or seeing the movie.

3. Students should cite parts of the book or movie that support their answers to question 2.

4. Students should write a short essay to persuade others to read the book or see the movie. They should present reasons why they enjoyed reading or seeing it and cite examples from the book or movie to support their reasons.

Page 25
Answers will vary, but students' paragraphs should explain an activity using a logical order of directions and sufficient detail.

Page 26
1. C
2. H
3. D
4. J
5. A
6. J
7. C
8. F
9. D
10. F
11. D

Page 27
1. Tyson began singing "The Star-Spangled Banner."
2. Joe read an article about Canadian geese in a magazine.
3. We sold school supplies to help raise money for the Red Cross.
4. "I'm really glad you are here," Abby said.
5. D
6. H
7. A
8. G

Page 28
1. a snowstorm
2. the night
3. mice
4. ice
5. kite

Answers will vary for 6–10. Some examples are:
6. a lunch as cold as ice
7. a friend like a sister
8. a coat as warm as a soft blanket
9. a winter day like a beautiful painting
10. with a smile that sparkled like sunshine

Page 29 Mini-Test 2
1. C
2. H
3. D
4. H
5. B
6. Horses can walk, trot, and gallop.
7. D
8. H
9. B

Page 30
1. Bats use echolocation to help them fly at night because they do not see well.

2. Students should note that breaking down the words into parts helps the reader to understand its meaning and how echolocation works.

3. Students should write two questions they have based on the passage.

4. Some possible resources include the library, Internet, and encyclopedias.

Page 31
1. B
2. G
3. A
4. G
5. C
6. F
7. A

Page 32
1. B
2. F
3. B
4. F
5. A
6. H
7. B
8. H

Page 33 Mini-Test 3
1. A
2. G
3. C
4. J
5. D
6. H
7. A

Page 34
1. f
2. a
3. c
4. h
5. g
6. d
7. e
8. b
9. b
10. d
11. a
12. c

Page 35
1. Students should list the book title.

2. Students should identify the genre.

3. Students should provide a summary of what the book is about.

4. Students should explain what their favorite part of the book is and why.

5. Students should explain what their least favorite part of the book is and why.

6. Students should critique how the author did in writing the book and explain their responses.
7. Students should share their book review with their friend and note how their answers were the same or different and why.

Page 36
Students' answers should tell about a personal experience and include details and feelings. It should have a beginning, middle, and end.

Page 37 Mini-Test 4
1. B
2. H
3. A
4. J
5. D
6. Students' answers should tell about their experiences and include details and feelings.

Pages 40–42 Final English Language Arts Test
1. C
2. G
3. B
4. H
5. C
6. H
7. A
8. H
9. C
10. H
11. A
12. J
13. C
14. G
15. B
16. F
17. B
18. F
19. C
20. G
21. C
22. G
23. A
24. F
25. B
26. J
27. B

Page 45
1. D
2. F
3. D
4. G
5. B
6. J
7. D
8. G

Page 46
1. C
2. F
3. D
4. H
5. D
6. G

Page 47
1. B
2. G
3. D
4. F
5. A
6. H
7. C
8. 3: 21, 27, 30
   4: 20, 24, 36
   G
9. 6: 42, 48, 66
   9: 18, 45, 54, 72
   A

Page 48
1. C
2. F
3. D
4. F
5. C
6. G
7. C
8. J
9. A
10. H

Page 49
1. 481
2. 786
3. 691
4. 884
5. 185
6. 190
7. 126
8. 173
9. 69
10. 16
11. 19
12. 27
13. 184
14. 264
15. 187
16. 565

Page 50
1. 7, 9; +2
2. 60, 40, 30; −10
3. 29, 36, 43; +7
4. 27, 24, 21, 18; −3
5. 70, 55, 40, 25; −15
6. 37, 28, 19, 10; −9
7. 41, 49, 57, 65; +8
8. 90, 72, 66, 60; −6
9. 77, 55, 33, 22; −11
10. 48, 60, 72, 84; +12
11. 50, 57, 64
12. 54, 48, 42

Page 51
1. variable: n (or any other letter)
   sentence: $3 + n = 9$
   solution: $n = 6$
2. variable: p (or any other letter)
   sentence: $4 + p = 13$
   solution: $p = 9$
3. variable: b (or any other letter)
   sentence: $314 \times 500 = b$
   solution: $b = \$157{,}000$
4. variable: k (or any other letter)
   sentence: $7 - 5 = k$
   solution: $k = 2$

Page 52
1. C
2. A
3. C
4. A
5. C
6. C
7. 3×4
8. $5 + 6 + 8$ or $8 + 6 + 5$
9. $(7 \times 4) \times 3$ or $4 \times (7 \times 3)$
10. $(4 \times 3) \times 7$ or $(3 \times 4) \times 7$ or $7 \times (3 \times 4)$
11. $8 + (4 + 2)$ or $(8 + 2) + 4$
12. $2 + (8 + 4)$ or $2 + (4 + 8)$ or $(4 + 8) + 2$

Page 53
1. 14
2. 29
3. Thursday
4. 100
5. Friday

Page 54
1. C
2. G
3. D
4. H

Page 55 Mini-Test 1
1. C
2. J
3. left
4. D
5. H
6. C
7. F
8. B
9. G
10. B
11. H

Page 56
1. parallelogram
2. rectangle
3. trapezoid
4. quadrilateral
5. square
6. parallelogram
7. quadrilateral
8. trapezoid
9. parallelogram

10. rectangle
11. trapezoid
12. trapezoid

Page 57
1. B
2. F
3. C
4. F
5. B
6. H

Page 58
1. boat
2. picnic basket
3. acorn
4. frog
5. butterfly
6. fish
7. worm
8. lily pad
9. flower
10. bird
11. leaf
12. rock
13–16. Check students' placement of items on graph.

Page 59
1. C
2. J
3. C
4. J

Page 60
Drawings will vary.

Page 61
1. b
2. a
3. d
4. e
5. c
6. c
7. e
8. a
9. d
10. b
11. d
12. c
13. a
14. b

Page 62
1. 21 feet
2. 2 feet
3. 2 yards
4. 52,800 feet
5. 5 feet
6. 32 quarts
7. 56 pints
8. 20 cups
9. 9 pints
10. 12 teaspoons
11. 6 gallons
12. 16 fluid ounces
13. 3 tablespoons
14. 32 tablespoons
15. 32 oz.
16. 10 lbs.
17. 240 oz.
18. 2 t.
19. 12,000 lbs.
20. 4 lbs.

Page 63
1. B
2. H
3. B
4. J
5. C
6. G
7. A
8. J

Page 64
1. height = 4,
   length = 4,
   width = 1,
   16 cubic units
2. height = 2,
   length = 3,
   width = 4,
   24 cubic units
3. height = 3,
   length = 3,
   width = 2,
   18 cubic units
4. height = 3,
   length = 2,
   width = 2,
   12 cubic units
5. height = 2,
   length = 5,
   width = 2,
   20 cubic units

Page 65 Mini-Test 2
1. B
2. F
3. B
4. F
5. B
6. J
7. C
8. G
9. A

Page 66
1.

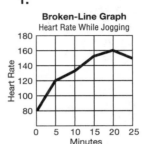

2.

3. 20 minutes
4. from 0 to 5 minutes
5. from 15 to 20 minutes
6. from 20 to 25 minutes

Page 67
1. D
2. G
3. A

Page 68
1. Answers will vary. Possible answer: 10 times for each number
2. Answers will vary. Possible answer: 30 times

3. Answers will vary. Possible answer: 30 times
4–9. Students should record their actual results.
10. Students should compare their results to the expected results.

Page 69
1. unlikely
2. unlikely
3. impossible
4. likely
5. likely
6. likely
7. likely
8. impossible
9. impossible
10. unlikely
11. certain
12. certain
13. impossible
14. impossible

Page 70
1. D
2. G
3. C
4. F
5. B
6. J
7. C

Page 71
1. D
2. H
3. B
4. G
5. A
6. 25 + 13 = 38
7. H
8. 47.82 − 25 = 22.82

Page 72
Students should describe how they solved each problem. Answers are:
1. 159 calories
2. $\frac{5}{8}$

3. 3 balloons
4. 23 cars
5. $15.00
6. $1.79

Page 73
1. D
2. G
3. C
4. G
5. B
6. J
7. C

Page 74 Mini-Test 3
1. D
2. H
3. C
4. G
5. C
6. G
7. $175 - 161 = 14$ or $2 \times 7 = 14$

Pages 76–78 Final Mathematics Test
1. C
2. J
3. A
4. J
5. D
6. J
7. C
8. F
9. B
10. H
11. B
12. H
13. B
14. H
15. B
16. J
17. A
18. G
19. A
20. H
21. B
22. F
23. B
24. G
25. C
26. H

Page 81
1. D
2. F
3. C
4. G
5. Answers will vary. One possible answer: American society highly values expressions of patriotism and love of country.

Page 82
1. C
2. Answers will vary. Students may state that a similarity is that many children today have chores or responsibilities at home. A difference might be that most American children today attend school.
3. J
4. C

Page 83
1. B
2. J
3. D
4. J
5. A

Page 84
1. Jonathan Smith; he is pleased with the Constitution, and thus approves of it.
2. Amos Singletary; he believes the wealthy will gain power under the Constitution and thus is against it.

Page 85
1. D
2. J
3. A
4. H
5. B

Page 86
1. B
2. J
3. A
4. H
5. C
6. G

Page 87
1. Each one shows a change in the moon or seasons, which occurs in patterns.
2. It is important to help understand and predict future events.
3. Students should describe changes that take place from one season to the next in the regions in which they live.
4. Answers will vary. One possible answer: Planning outdoor events would be nearly impossible if weather patterns were not somewhat predictable.

Page 88 Mini-Test 1
1. C
2. H
3. D
4. J
5. B
6. H
7. D

Page 89
1. Answers will vary. Students should describe their community, including as many details as possible.
2. Answers will vary. Students should describe their home, including as many details as possible.

Page 90
Answers will vary. Students should identify two groups that they are a part of and describe how each group has affected the way they live or act.

Pages 91–92
1. B
2. H
3. A
4. H
5. D
6. G
7. A
8. They fought the hijackers and prevented the plane from crashing into another building, probably saving hundreds of lives.
9. Answers will vary. One possible answer: Schools helped explain the situation to America's children and gave them a place to talk about what was going on.

Page 93 Mini-Test 2
1. Answers will vary. Students should describe in detail one of the members of their family.

2. Answers will vary. Students should describe one thing they have learned about how to act or live from that family member.
3. D
4. G
5. C

Page 94
1. C
2. J
3. C
4. H
5. A
6. G
7. C
8. G
9. D
10. F

Page 95
1. C
2. G
3. C
4. J
5. B
6. G

Page 96
1. C
2. J
3. C
4. F
5. B

Page 97
1. C
2. H
3. A
4. G
5. A
6. J
7. Answers will vary. One possible answer: People wanted to purchase the generators because they needed another source for their electricity. They were willing to pay a higher price since their normal source of electricity was unavailable.

Page 98
1. C
2. F
3. B
4. J
5. B
6. H
7. C

Page 99
1. A
2. G
3. A
4. G
5. B
6. H

Page 100 Mini-Test 3
1. D
2. G
3. D
4. H
5. B
6. J
7. C
8. J

Pages 101–102
1. A
2. G
3. D
4. H
5. A
6. Answers will vary. One possible answer: Crops may be able to be grown in what were once cooler areas. Other areas may experience draught. Some areas may not be able to grow enough food to feed those living there.

7. Answers will vary. One possible answer: The student will contribute more to global warming by using more machines, such as computers, microwaves, cars, etc. These machines in turn use energy that contributes to greenhouse gases. The mother may raise livestock that emit methane gas, but this probably has a smaller impact.
8. Answers will vary. Students might list walking or riding a bike instead of riding in a car, recycling to avoid placing more items in a landfill, turning off appliances such as computers, TVs, and lamps when not in use, dressing more warmly and turning the heat down at home, and waiting to do laundry until a full load is available.

Page 103
1. C
2. J
3. Answers will vary. One possible answer: Voters have a responsibility to understand the issues and know where the candidates stand on them before voting.

4. Answers will vary. One possible answer: It benefits the accused by ensuring that he or she receives a fair trial.
5. Students' responses will vary. They should rank the rights shown from most to least important to them personally, then explain their rankings.

Page 104
Students' paragraphs will vary but should describe how the rights to life, liberty, and the pursuit of happiness are applicable to people's lives today.

Page 105 Mini-Test 4
1. C
2. J
3. B
4. H
5. Answers will vary. One possible answer: William has the right to free speech, which Jane did not respect by trying to stop his actions. William respected others' views by not forcing his booklet onto them if they were not interested.

Pages 108–110 Final Social Studies Test
1. A
2. J
3. B
4. F
5. C
6. H
7. B

8. F
9. B
10. J
11. B
12. H
13. A
14. J
15. D
16. G
17. C
18. G
19. D
20. H
21. C
22. J
23. B
24. J
25. C
26. G

Page 114
1. Yes. The passage confirms that *hydro* refers to water, so *hydropower* refers to power that comes from water.
2. A
3. J
4. A

Page 115
1. C
2. F
3. B
4. G
5. A
6. J
7. C
8. F

Page 116
Students should mention that Terry did his second experiment a month later, in September, which meant the plants received less sunlight than the ones in the first experiment. He may have forgotten to take this factor into account when repeating his study.

Page 117 Mini-Test 1
1. D
2. F
3. C
4. G
5. C
6. H
7. D
8. J

Page 118
1. C
2. J
3. C
4. F
5. C
6. G
7. B
8. J

Page 119
1. P
2. V
3. C
4. P
5. C
6. V
7. P
8. C
9. V
10. P

Page 120
1. B
2. H
3. B
4. H
5. A
6. G
7. C
8. F
9. C
10. H

Page 121
1. A
2. J
3. C
4. H
5. B
6. G
7. C
8. F

Page 122
1. D
2. G
3. A
4. G
5. Answers will vary. One possible answer: Most of the desert plants and animals, such as cacti and reptiles, might die because they are accustomed to warmer temperatures.
6. Answers will vary. One possible answer: Animals and plants that are used to cooler temperatures might thrive. These organisms might have trouble finding food if their usual sources die off in the colder environment.
7. Only the most heat-resistant plants and animals would survive. Forests might be replaced by deserts.

Page 123
1. C
2. G
3. C
4. F
5. D

Page 124
1. A
2. H
3. B
4. H
5. B
6. J
7. A
8. F
9. A
10. J

Page 125
1. C
2. J
3. A
4. F
5. A
6. G
7. C

Page 126
1. A
2. G
3. D
4. F
5. B
6. J
7. B
8. H
9. A
10. H

Page 127 Mini-Test 2
1. D
2. G
3. A
4. F
5. C
6. G
7. C
8. G
9. C

Page 128
1. B
2. G
3. A
4. F
5. A
6. Answers will vary. One possible answer: A scientist may communicate findings to other scientists via a computer e-mail message.
7. Answers will vary. One possible answer: Heart monitors have allowed doctors to keep better track of their patients' health.

Page 129
1. A
2. H
3. D
4. F
5. C
6. J

Page 130
1. C
2. F
3. D
4. J
5. D
6. F
7. A
8. J

Page 131 Mini-Test 3
1. D
2. F
3. B
4. J
5. B
6. H
7. B
8. J
9. B
10. F

Pages 133–135 Final Science Test
1. A
2. H
3. B
4. J
5. C
6. G
7. A
8. H
9. B
10. F
11. B
12. H
13. D
14. G
15. A
16. J
17. D
18. J
19. D
20. H
21. B

22. G
23. A
24. H
25. B
26. G
27. D